J. CASTELLAR-GASSOL

PICASSO
The 7 lives of the artist

Edicions de 1984
Barcelona

Picasso, Les 7 vides de l'artista
© Joan Castellar-Gassol

First edition: July 2006

Design: Enric Satué
© Sucesión Pablo Picasso, VEGAP, Barcelona, 2006
© Man Ray, VEGAP, Barcelona, 2006
© Robert Capa, MAGNUM/CONTACTO
© Antonio Cores: Reserved Rigths
The autors of the other photographs are unknown to the publishers,
Who welcome any information regarding their ownership
© for this edition, 2006 by Edicions de 1984, s.l.
Pujades, 74-80 - 08005 Barcelona
E-mail: 1984@edicions1984.cat
www.edicions1984.cat

Printed in Catalonia

ISBN: 84-96061-71-X
Legal deposit: B. 30.832-2006

«¡What a great artist you would be
if only you painted like Rembrandt!»

OLGA KOKLOVA, *Picasso's first wife*

«The Museu Picasso of Barcelona is
the most important in the world of its genre»

JOAN CORTÈS (1898-1969),
Art history professor in Llotja

Summary

PART ONE

1

Petit Louis could have never imagined that the portrait painted of him by a foreign painter who lived in Paris would gain world fame.

Louis was a poor French boy with a reputation as a petty thief who lived in the Parisian district Montmartre, and who, one day at the beginning of the 20th century, was paid four badly counted coins to be a model for the foreign painter who scraped a living painting portraits. This seemingly insignificant occurrence, featuring two individuals who at the beginning of the 1900's were completely unknown, suddenly surfaces a century later, in May 2004, when the oil on canvas portrait of young Louïs, dusted off and finely framed, was sold at auction in Sotheby's of New York for nearly $100,000,000.00 (one hundred million dollars).

Never had such a colossal amount been paid for a painting, and the first one who would have been surprised and maybe even scandalized is the painter himself, Pablo Picasso, in the improbable case that he had survived to see it. Wall Street's financial sector is more than usually motivated by rising art prices, but

John Richardson, Picasso's loyal biographer and enthusiast of his work, declared: «The buyer would have done better to have destined the grotesque amount of money to something more beneficial for humanity.»

The global fame that now surrounds the name of Picasso is the result of various circumstances, not all of them artistic. He was a boy who began to speak later than usual, who had difficulties with letters and numbers in primary school, but who, on the other hand, possessed an innate ability for drawing. As an adolescent he was considered a precocious artist. This is demonstrated by the oil painting entitled *Ciència i Caritat* («Science and Charity», Museu Picasso of Barcelona), which represents a young dying mother, accompanied by a doctor and a nun. This piece received a well-deserved mention of honour in the Fine Arts Exhibition of Madrid in the year 1897.

Although a trained eye may notice an error in the perspective of the composition, the treatment of the figures is impeccable. Incidentally, it was Picasso's father who posed as a model for the doctor.

More than the artist's abilities, however, what attracted the attention of the stiff academics of the Castilian capital's artistic circles was the age of the artist Pablo Picasso: at just 16 he was a young dark haired man of short stature, big ears and small hands with thick fingers, lively eyes and an intelligent expression.

This young and talented painter's dedication to art came from his father, an Andalusian named José Ruiz

Portrait of María Picasso López,
mother of the artist. Barcelona, 1896

Blasco, painter and teacher of classical drawing, married to María Picasso López, of Genovese origin on her father's side.

The first child of the couple, Pablo Ruiz Picasso, was born on October 25th 1881 in a house located in the central Merced Square in Malaga (Andalusia), into a reasonably well off family with a modest income, but still employing domestic servants, as was expected of all the homes of gentlemen, or «señoritos» according to established Andalusian tradition.

Within the family there was a tradition that members followed respectable careers in official or ecclesiastical professions. The deceased Monsignor Pablo Ruiz Blasco, José Ruiz Blasco's brother, and therefore, the young painter's uncle had been a canon of the cathedral and it was he who gave his name to the newborn child. Another one of José's brothers was the «Head Doctor of the port's health section» while Doña María Picasso's distant cousin had chosen a military career and reached the rank of general in the Spanish army.

José was a teaching assistant in painting and drawing at the «Provincial School of Fine Arts», a restorer of antique paintings, and also the curator of the «Provincial Museum of Malaga». However, official salaries did not allow much leeway, especially in traditional large families which were common, and particularly in the Ruiz-Picasso family, where a multitude of parents, children, aunts and uncles and close and distant cousins all lived together.

Malaga, which boasts Phoenician foundations on the Mediterranean coast, at the turn of the 19th century had notable architectural remnants of the Muslim occupation, as well as numerous Christian convents. The city, which then had some 100,000 inhabitants, experienced periods of agricultural, industrial and commercial prosperity, but in the 1880s it was declining in importance in the eyes of the world.

To the numerous churches, convents, chapels and hermitages, we can add the Baroque imagery, sculptures, paintings on canvas backed with wood and rich altarpieces. At every saints festival the city's traditions and history were celebrated, a custom which in a large part derived from the period of the Catholic Kings at the end of the 15th century and beginning of the 16th, when monarchs from Castilla and Aragón eliminated the last

The father of the artist.
Barcelona, 1896

Muslim stronghold of the Iberian peninsula, as well as expelling the Jewish population, making way for a triumphant Catholicism and, in consequence, the spread of the grandiose Baroque style.

Religious brotherhoods were numerous, processions were fantastic and the «Plaza de Toros» was always filled when there were bullfights, which was quite often. However agricultural exports were declining, the Phyloxera plague was extending through the south of the peninsula and a cholera epidemic was beginning to wreak havoc. Many historic buildings showed the scars of time and negligence. The walls and towers of Alcazaba, an ancient palace of the Moorish period, were in ruins, while at the edge of the markets the fish vendors were showing increasing signs of hunger. The few industries that did exist were in crisis and teachers were sometimes paid their salary months late. As if this wasn't enough, an earth-quake destroyed around one hundred houses and the Ruiz Picassos were forced to take refuge in the home of a neighbouring friend, Antonio Muñoz Degrain, a grand master of historic painting.

In spite of everything, the Ruiz-Picasso family was growing in size. In 1884 they had a girl who was baptised with the name of Dolores (Lola as she was called in the family) and in 1887 another girl was born who was given the name of Concepción. Four years later, when a future in Malaga appeared impossible, the father decided to emigrate with his wife and all the children to A Coruña (Galicia), where he was offered one job as a drawing teacher in a secondary school and another in the local Fine Arts School.

It was there, in the multicoloured but socially decay-ing baroque environment of Malaga where the infant Pablo Ruiz Picasso had his first experiences of life. Re-membering them, he told a friend and admirer (Josep Palau i Fabre) that the school and religious ceremonies bored him, but that, on the other hand, he loved watch-ing the bullfights. It seems that he was being sincere as it is precisely the symbol of the bull - for most tourists the symbol or «logo» of Spain - that appears as a *leitmotif* throughout Picasso's work. The symbol is commonly as-sociated with the Minotaur, the mythic insatiable mon-ster with a bull's head and a human body, to whom the mythical King Minos offered seven virgins to calm his ire.

2

A Coruña was hardly the ideal destination for Pablo Picasso. The move from the Mediterranean beaches of translucent luminosity to the humid and misty Atlantic coast of Galicia, from the open and casual character of the Andalusians to the reserved and serious character of the Galicians, and from the Moorish tones of the Andalusian dialect to the Galician language with its Celtic sounds was not easy to adapt to. The salary of Sr José Ruiz may have improved but the young Picasso had a hard time in the lessons his father gave him at the Fine Arts School. His instinct for the arts kept him drawing and painting, but the academic rules and regulations were difficult to accept.

Sr José Ruiz, sickly and depressed, still saw little hope for the future and motivated with the wave of interest created by the success of the 1888 Universal Exhibition in Barcelona, packed his bags once again and moved with the entire family to the Catalonian capital, at the time considered the most advanced and powerful of the Iberian peninsula.

A family tragedy could have been the final push for

José's abandonment of Galicia. His daughter Concepción, the third child, died of diphtheria at the age of 7. Before the year had finished, the Ruiz Picassos had settled in the Catalonian capital. There, with a backdrop of chimney smoke, electrical explosions, the noise of the trams, the grand palaces of the Universal Exhibition, the grids of bourgeoisie houses and the rows of slouching workers who, wearing espadrilles, kept the furnaces alight; the explosive phase of the Industrial Revolution was taking place.

The Spanish empire was agonised: the colonies of Puerto Rico, the Philippines and Cuba had taken up arms against the metropolis, a fact that frustrated Madrid's forces but gave hope to Catalonian families. If the colonial wars were to finish, their children could return home. Furthermore, a large part of Catalonian society hoped to recover some of the ancient liberties that the Catalonian Principality and the Crown of Aragón had previously enjoyed, in a similar vein to the aspirations of freedom, autonomy and independence that boiled in Ireland and other European countries. All together, Barcelona had become a city of social agitations, both civic and non-civic, a laboratory for new and daring experiences and a sounding box for all the novelties that came from Paris.

Crazy inventiveness, proletarian misery, anti-social ideology, revolutionary desires, adversarial spirits and a delirium of innovation dominated the city where Pablo Ruiz Picasso lead an intermittently irregular life between

Málaga, 1894

the ages of 14 and 23. The first summer that he spent in Barcelona, a bomb attack launched by anarchists against the devotees participating in a procession along Canvis Nous Street during the Corpus Christi festivities killed a dozen people. During his penultimate year in the city, he was witness to the city coming to a complete standstill due to a general strike of a kind never seen before.

Despite the inherent individualism in artists' characters, not all felt detached from the social uproar. The inimitable and always elegant painter Ramón Casas, in his work *La Càrrega* («The Charge», Olot Museum), has immortalised the attack by civil guards with unsheathed swords on horses, against workers who protested with their hands in their pockets asking for bread and justice. Isidre Nonell, who drew caricatures of the poor on the streets of Barcelona, left us testimonies which today are historical documents, such as the work *La Misèria*

(«Misery», Museo de Arte Moderno de Barcelona, MNAC). Joaquim Mir painted the *La Catedral dels Pobres* («The Cathedral of the Poor», Buxeres collection) which depicts the emotional scene of a begging mother with her son in her arms, against the backdrop of the works on the Sagrada Familia directed by the architect Antoni Gaudi.

Artistic works such as these, particularly those of Nonell and Mir, could not be ignored by a lively spirit like Pablo Picasso and the impression that these two Catalonian artists left on Picasso is highly visible in his early work.

In the midst of citizen agitation, there were still some peaceful oases, one of which was the Barcelona School of Fine Arts, established in the 18th century in the stately Llotja (stock exchange) building on the edge of the Maritime Walk. The imposing neo-classical style of the exterior and the gothic hall of the interior, with its perfect geometry, suggested the platonic ideal of the palaces visited by the muses, where beauty resides. It was in this privileged space that Picasso's father had achieved a placement as a drawing teacher and where he had managed to enrol his talented son as a student.

His father, a sensible, conservative and mature man, rigorously followed the current academic painting rules, which had changed little since the Renaissance period, and his son attempted to follow the desires and instructions of his father as well as he could. He had still not turned 14 when he painted *Vell Pescador* («Old Fisherman», Museu de Montserrat, Catalonia), a lively realist oil portrait on canvas. He was 14 or 15 when he did a portrait in profile with pastels on paper, *La Madre del Artista* («Mother of the Artist», Museu Picasso, Barcelona), small in size (50cm), luminous and excellently executed. At 15 years of age he exhibited his first great academic canvas in the Barcelona Fine Arts Exhibition, *La Primera Comunió* («First Communion», Museu Picasso, Barcelona). At 16 he received his first honourable mention in the Madrid Fine Arts Exhibition and a gold medal in Malaga for *Ciència i Caritat*.

But, in spite of the influences that he was receiving from the Llotja School as well as from other Catalonian artists, in Picasso's soul there burned desires that were bursting to come out. The opportunity to begin to release them came when fate lead him to spend a season in an isolated corner of Catalonia, far from the great city.

3

By the often surprising and invisible law of selective affinities, Picasso, at 14 years of age and of short stature, became friends with Manuel Pallarès, a school mate in Llotja School who was 5 years older and as tall as a giant.

Son of a land owner in Horta, a village next to the mountains of Ports de Beseit, about 80 km southwest of Tarragona, the corpulent Pallarès showed a sincere and protective affection towards the Andalusian youth. The Catalonian guided him through the dark medieval streets in the centre of Barcelona. They went to cheap taverns and cafés together where music-hall dancers moved their bodies in an imitation of the Parisian Moulin Rouge dancers, and there they made notes, as they knew the Parisian painters such as Toulouse-Lautrec had done.

The camaraderie between the painter from Malaga and the Catalonian was strengthened, when, in the summer of 1898, Picasso returned from a wasted visit to Madrid. He had promised his family that he would study seriously, but he didn't. Lacking stimulus, he did not take advantage of the teachings that the great master

Horta de Sant Joan

Muñoz Degrain gave in the Academia de San Fernando. He had gone to the Prado Museum which he only knew from a quick visit before arriving in Barcelona and he had made a copy of the portrait of Phillip 4th by Velázquez, (Museu Picasso, Barcelona). It is possible that the exuberant colour variations of the important works of the Prado museum, from leaden white to the transparent emerald greens, yellows, carmines and Venetian reds, inhibited him more than they inspired. Whatever the problem had been, he had wasted his time and his family stopped sending him money. Feeling alone, he fell ill and returned emaciated and crestfallen to Barcelona.

Pallarès, feeling sorry for him, invited him to spend some time at his summer home in Horta where he could rebuild his life.

The village of Horta and its surroundings were then

little known, or ignored, by the majority of city dwellers. Steep mountains with inaccessible ravines alternate with narrow border passes, and wild goats rule the land. The palmetto, a beautiful native tree, adds a certain beauty to areas of brush and wonderful pines provide shade on the plateaus near the hills. Crystalline streams flow down the hillsides and at the base of some of them remains of the ash and lava left by a volcanic cataclysm in the primitive eras of the earth can still be found.

Horta, filled with medieval houses, predominately from the 16th century, is situated on top of a hill of primitive geological formation. The big stone houses, with their hugely thick walls, are piled up next to each other, or on top of one another, following the winding roads that curve up and down and taking advantage of the corners to poke out above the rest, like plants that battle to stick their heads out and receive the sun's vital rays in a lush forest. And like the roots from the huge trees that penetrate the earth's belly, the ground floor of the Casa de la Vila, located in the church square, has deep cellars that perforate the underground rock and which, in ancient times, served as prisons.

Picasso, who knew only the stone paved towns of Malaga, A Coruña, Madrid and Barcelona, would stay in Horta and the surrounding area from the summer of 1898 to February 1899 where he would have the opportunity to live unforgettable experiences. According to the memoirs of M. Pallarès, which have been written by the Picasso scholar J. Palau i Fabre, the two went up to

Ports de Beseit with a mule loaded with painting materials, a blanket and food. In certain places, they had to cut their way through the bushes with a knife and be careful not to fall into holes or deep water, as happened to Picasso who rolled down a hill and into such a pond. Picasso, who didn't know how to swim, was saved by his strong friend's quick thinking. Their camping adventure was short but saw many incidents including violent winds which extinguished their fire or knocked down the canvases that they had set up.

On their return to Horta, Picasso stayed with the Pallarès for a further six months, during which he occasionally helped with rural tasks such as feeding the animals, loading manure into the donkeys saddlebags, cleaning the stables, saddling the mules, pulling up water from the well or helping the women of the house knead the dough to make bread. J. Palau i Fabre says that «At Els Ports Picasso lived the life of primitive man», and that during the stay with the Pallarès «he was very interested in rural work and would often stop to contemplate and ask questions. It was where his Catalan, badly learned in Barcelona, was perfected. He liked to watch the locksmith, the saddle maker, the shoemaker and the farmer working on their trades, an interest that remained captured in a series of quick notes».

Some Catalonian authors proudly state that Picasso, as an adult and at the height of his fame would have said: «All I know, I have learned in Horta». Whether this anecdote is true or not, it is certain that the healthy experiences of the farmer's life had restored his vitality. He returned to Barcelona with drawings and a painting under his arm, a small landscape entitled *El Mas del Quiquet* («The Country House of Quiquet», Museu Picasso, Barcelona), the impressionist tone of which, although a hint rather than a fully fledged style, suggested that from now on he would take different paths, rather more grim than the those of the woodland beauty of Ports de Beseit. The first stop on the journey was, without a doubt, the Catalonian capital.

4

Picasso's parents had helped their son to pay the rent for one of the first workshops that he used in Barcelona for the creation of his first works. They could not, however, do much more, and the boy had to make do on his own, sharing various workshops with other artists, almost all from well off families, and asking questions of as many people as possible in an effort to establish himself. If he had breathed in high class culture without benefiting from it at the Llotja school, the workshops and the winding roads of the ancient city captured the silent presence of the miserable, and he felt a fatal attraction to the depths, where female workers in the oldest trade in the world mixed with the rich clients of the bourgeoisie, anarchists with fiery ideas, opium smokers, artists with mystic inclinations, tortured psychology souls and robust thugs who hid knives in their sashes.

Besides Manuel Pallarès, another character that served as a guide for Picasso in the slums of Barcelona and the surrounding area was Juli Vallmitjana. Eight years older than Picasso, Vallmitjana was from a rich silversmith's family. Dedicated to literature and fascinated by the world of the gypsies, he earned the trust of some of them above all of a thug who served as his body guard, and had learnt slang and the caló tongue. According to J. Palau i Fabre, «Picasso ventured by night, into Gracia, an industrial district added to Barcelona in 1897, in the company of Vallmitjana. It was risky to go out at night, but Vallmitjana knew the thugs of the area and on giving his name, he was respected and could circulate freely».

Not everything was excursions and walks in the slums. On June 13th 1902, the poet priest Jacinto Verdaguer, the glory of Catalan literature, was buried in the Montjuic cemetery. A group of regulars at the bar «Els Quatre Gats», among whom was Picasso, added themselves to the lengthy mourning retinue and left a bouquet of flowers on the coffin.

The fact that Picasso was a student of the prestigious Llotja school, that he had won an honorary prize in Madrid and that he demonstrated extreme ease in sketching a person's profile or a street scene in a few strokes, had attracted the attention of a select trio of veteran painters made up of Santiago Rusiñol, Ramon Casas and Miquel Utrillo who had lived and worked in Paris which was then the most important centre for the Fine Arts.

Miquel Utrillo had been to Paris when he was 18 years old. Santiago Rusiñol went in 1888, when he was 27 years old and painting in the style of Degas and

Whistler, and had visited Catalonia from time to time. His close friend Ramon Casas followed him two years later, but Casas, who was highly gifted, had already had his first resounding success in Paris. At 13, Casas worked as an assistant to a Barcelona painting teacher. At 16 he did the same for a French teacher in Paris, with whom he worked with for a year. At 17, one of his self portraits was accepted for hanging in the Salon des Artistes Français of the French capital. Casas, Rusiñol and Utrillo lived in Montmartre, in rented rooms in the later famous Moulin de le Galette. Renoir painted the interior in 1876 and Rusiñol, later, painted the exterior.

This was the golden age of the cafe gatherings. There were many in Barcelona, but Rusiñol, Casas and Utrillo, with a desire for a space that was their own, had opened a place in 1897 that was a mix between cabaret and bar on Montsió Street, not far from the cathedral. The imposing shadow of the ancient and now closed monastery, a biblical memory of Mount Sion in Jerusalem that gave the street its name, contributed to making the place extremely dark, but the building that was chosen to for the new enterprise was, and still is, a beautiful building in the up and coming style of the time, called «modernist» in Catalonia and «Art Nouveau» in France, although the aesthetic originated in England.

The Frenchified aesthetes and promoters of the new bar gave it a name which was a mixture of irony and elitism, «Els Quatre Gats» (The Four Cats). The name imitated the Parisian Cabaret «Chat Noir» (Black Cat) as well as making reference to the fact that they expected few clients - the common and slightly vulgar Catalonian expression «som quatre gats» (we're are only four cats) means precisely that - «to be just a few».

The International Exhibition in Paris in 1900 had solidified the fame of the modernist style, and to coincide, the «Four Cats» showed a small exhibition of drawings and paintings by different artists. Picasso was invited to exhibit some of his art works. One of them, a drawing for a poster that was no bigger than 30cm, coloured with simple colours, represented, with rapid clear lines, clients sitting at the tables in front of the establishment. The bar owner used the poster on the menu of the place and since then, many reproductions have been made.

The veterans of the gathering encouraged Picasso to continue with his clear, suggestive lines, but his dark instinct pushed him in a different direction which he wanted to explore in Paris.

»Paris, Rome and Barcelona formed the original triangle, geographically and historically, of the Western world» said the historian Sir J.W. Headlam-Morley and, significantly, Rome and Paris were leaders in the Fine Arts, to which Barcelona, and the rest of Catalonia, made an important contribution.

In the mid 19th century, there were still artists that were guided by Rome's leadership, where the fabulous Greek-Roman legacy was revitalised by the Renaissance artist Giorgio Vasari, who had said: «let no artist ever dream of perfecting a painting or chiselling marble with more skill and grace than Michael Angelo Buonarroti, because in his work the sum of the value and the power of art can be seen».

Some front line Catalonians had worked in Rome before its absorption by the Unified Italian State. The exceptional neoclassic sculptor Damià Campeny had worked in the Vatican's workshops.

The Malagan genius of paint, Marià Fortuny, also precociously gifted and who sadly died before her time at the age of 36 in Rome, left the city of the Popes a mature work that, in many ways, has never been surpassed. Marià Fortuny had said, in the year 1858, that the city was «a great cemetery visited by foreigners», but at the end of the century, there were still Catalonian painters like the expert Enric Sierra i Auqué, who worked in Rome where he died in 1918.

The Roman decline was unstoppable as the war that ended in the creation of the Italian State took hold. At the turn of the 20th century, almost all artists looked to the French capital where the mastery of the drawings of Ingres, who died in 1867, reminded them that the classic canon was impossible to surpass. But it was precisely in Paris where clever dealers knew how to commercialise and export modern painting all over the world.

A new century had begun in 1900, the century of marvels, if one listens to the optimists. And in the autumn of that inaugural year, Picasso arrived in Paris as if to the capital of the world.

5

The Eiffel tower captured, in forged iron, the idea of constant, unstoppable material progress, the fashionable ideology of the end of the 19th century and the beginning of the 20th. Its height, some 320m, made it the highest monument in Europe. Paris lay at its feet, and together with the Universal Exhibition of 1900, it offered the world a spectacle of inventiveness, power, barely concealed Napoleonic nostalgia and the hegemonic ambition of the French State.

In a charcoal drawing, Picasso had sketched a scene in which he and four other Catalonian painters are happily leaving the Universal Exhibition arm in arm. Picasso represents himself as a dwarf, maybe to exaggerate his short stature, next to Ramon Pitxot, who is depicted as very tall, together with Ramon Casas, Miquel Utrillo, Carles Casagemas and an attractive girl.

The artists, the majority foreigners, were established in areas of Montmartre and Montparnasse, and lived a neglectful bohemian life, golden in the case of the rich and miserable in the case of the poor, a kind of voluntary ghetto. The Dreyfus issue was still alive and kicking with confrontation between anti-Semitic conservatives and radical socialists and a certain turbulence was present in official circles. Few months had passed since the president of the republic, Félix Faure, had died under strange circumstances. It was rumoured that he had been assassinated. Everything appeared under control, but no one had forgotten that just a few years back, between 1893 and 1894, the anarchists had committed more than fifty attacks. The most spectacular of these was the bomb that was thrown into the chamber of the Members of Parliament, and the stabbing to death of the previous president of the republic Sadi Carnot.

The favoured district of the foreign artists was Montmartre, where Toulouse Lautrec captured on canvas the rhythms of the can-can, danced at the Moulin Rouge music-hall. The painters that arrived from Catalonia visited the place when they could, sometimes invited by the owner and founder of the establishment, Josep Oller, another Catalonian.

Paris, the «Ville Lumière» of over two million inhabitants, was made for strong spirits. The weak would fall along the way, as did Picasso's friend Carles Casagemas. They were almost the same age and Casagemas had travelled to France with Picasso the first time around. Admirer of expressionist and symbolical paintings, with a problematic character and lacking in life experience, he fell madly in love with the first girl he met in the French capital. She was a very lively woman, who made everyone call her Germaine, but her real name was Laura

Gargallo and she was the wife of Ramon Pichot, an excellent Catalonian painter trained in Paris. Be it because Casagemas was impotent or whatever the reason, love turned into frustration and on February 17th 1901, he tried to kill the woman of his dreams with a gun. At the last moment he changed his mind, turned the firearm on himself and committed suicide.

When Picasso, who had already returned to Spain, heard news of the tragedy, his confusion and congenital melancholy deepened. Some experts on his work say that Casagemas' suicide marked a decided change in his work which lasted for the next three years. Almost monochromatic canvases, in dark blue, represent disturbed figures immersed in despair.

Even so, the expert, Marilyn McCully, author of in depth studies on Picasso, states that colour was never his strong feature, whereas drawing was, and that he had a tendency to monochromatic paintings. Another expert, André Fermigier, has reminded us that the paintings from this era, which has been called the «blue period», are very similar to the Catalonian painter Isidre Nonell's work, and clearly symbolic in inspiration.

Picasso was depressed but he could not stop working rigorously because he had to live, and in order to do so, had to deliver the paintings that he had promised to a Catalonian dealer that he had met in Paris, Pere Manyac, with whom he also shared a flat.

Showing a paternal spirit, Miquel Utrillo (not to be confused with the Frenchman Maurice Utrillo), who was twenty years older than Picasso, wanted to encourage him and dedicated an article to him signed «Pinzell» (Paint Brush) in the *Pèl i Ploma* Barcelona Magazine. The article was titled «*Dibuixos d'en Picasso*» (Picasso's Drawings). The young Malagan, who felt greater sentimental ties to his mother than his father, had decided, whilst living in Paris, to keep only his mother's name, which also sounded more original to Spanish ears. From then on he signed «Pablo R. Picasso». With time, however, the R. in his name was also dropped and from then on he was known as Pablo Picasso.

«Although Picasso has not taken advantage of the strict lessons of the Llotja school in Barcelona, he has seen the work of many painters that know how to paint without having to go to official schools», Utrillo wrote in the Barcelona magazine. «Some of the works of the young Andalusian painter, exhibited in Els Quatre Gats, were quickly acquired by those that were searching for the early fruits of art ... Picasso's art is fruit of a spirit of observation that does not forgive the weaknesses of the people of our time, and in which beauty can be seen in the most horrible things...In this issue of the magazine *Pèl i Ploma* we publish some of his drawings which show the quickness of the young painter's vision, not yet 20 years old, and who is called *Little Goya* by his French friends».

There are two of Picasso's drawings from those years that not only are of a great beauty and show a moving intensity, but are also really surprising when one sees how his work went on to develop into the complete opposite of its first beginnings. The fact that they show the influence of the muted colours of the artworks being painted by the Swedish and Norwegians at the time does not reduce their merit. The two drawings mentioned are «*A la fi del camí*» («The end of the road», Thannhauser collection, New York) a watercolour and pastel work from 1898 and «*La boja*» («The Madwoman»), a drawing (published in the magazine «Juventud» of Barcelona in 1900). Also noteworthy is his large oil on canvas, «*Le Moulin de la Galette*» 1900 («The Galette Windmill», Solomon R. Guggenheim Museum, New York).

In June 1901, around sixty of Picasso's paintings and drawings had been exhibited in the gallery of the rascal but efficient French dealer Ambriose Vollard. More than half were sold and the specialist press took notice. The police wanted to know who this young foreign painter who dressed like a tramp was and who he was socialising with. A police report dated June 18th of that year states: «Having arrived in Paris on May 5th, Picasso has since been staying at the house of his fellow countryman, the anarchist Pierre Manach who is under our supervision, at No. 130, Clichy Boulevard...He goes out every night with his friend, returns very late and, sometimes sleeps elsewhere». The concierge of the building told the police that «she had never heard him utter a single subversive word», although she added that «he speaks French so badly that one could hardly understand him». This and the theme of his paintings, seen by a police inspector, caused the district commissioner to arrive at the following conclusion: «From the preceding report we can conclude that Picasso shares the ideas of his fellow countryman Manach with whom he is staying, and therefore should be considered an anarchist».

A year later, in December 1902, his work, which he had since managed to exhibit more than once in Paris, caught the attention of Charles Morice, a consummate art critic for the prestigious magazine *Mercure de France* in which he wrote: «The sterile sadness that weighs down the work is extraordinary, even in the plentiful work of the young Picasso, who started to paint before he learned how to read. The hundreds of faces that he has painted grimace. Not a single one is smiling. He represents a world as uninhabitable as the factories that are plagued by leprosy. His painting is sick». And thinking of *Les Fleurs du mal* of Baudelaire, he ended with a somewhat premonitory question: «Like a Flower of Evil, with his head full of desperate or criminal thoughts, is this precocious young boy destined to paint a master piece based on the negative in life?»

That such an important magazine as *Mercure de France,* founded by Chateaubriand in the mid 19th century had paid attention to the unknown artist, was an sure sign that Picasso was starting to awaken interest in the world of art dealers, collectors, critics and other artists. Picasso, on the other hand, had earned little at

Vollard's, the majority of the earnings must have ended up in the pockets of Pere Manyac and Monsenior Vollard. It seems, however, that the greediest of all the dealers with whom Picasso had dealings with was Clovis Sagot, a former circus clown and dubious character who established a sleazy gallery in a former Parisian pharmacy.

The collectors were of a different type and obviously had a different outlook. One of the first collectors who had the instinct to show interest in Picasso and who had been doing so since 1901, was Olivier Sainsière, who had a high level position as state advisor in the French administration.

Among the many influences on Picasso, the one that stands out the most is the Catalonian Isidre Nonell, whose style caused a special obsession in Picasso. Nonell, who had been influenced by the Swiss poster artist Théophile A. Steinlen, who worked for the anarchists, was the son of a pasta maker and had studied at the Llotja school of Barcelona, but early on developed an interest in capturing figures which were deformed or odd. In the beginning, in Barcelona, the critics turned their backs on him, but in Paris, where he exhibited some artwork, he was appreciated. A critic from the *Revue des Beaux Arts* said the following about him: «with his knowledge of how to capture the Horrible, he achieves a strange impression of grandeur».

Between Nonell and Picasso there are evident parallels. The former had gone to a sanatorium in Valle de

Boí, a wooded region of the Pyrenees, where there were mentally ill patients, rickets sufferers, degenerates, those deformed by an endemic illness caused by the inbreeding of the population. Nonell had done a huge number of drawings that were exhibited, in 1897, at the *Salon du Champ-de-Mars* in Paris. «He noticed the men that had the most repugnant aspect and he reproduced them, with a kind of sadistic fever», Carolina Nonell, niece of the artist and art specialist, wrote. «He searched for that dispossessed humanity that we contemplate with indifference or contempt and he observed it lovingly».

Picasso, on the other hand, had, between the years 1901 and 1902, visited the Women's Prison of Saint-Lazare of Paris several times. The place was filled with delinquents, prostitutes and the crazy, and a few poor women with children in their arms. Some of the notes and sketches that he made of the recluses were later used to paint oils in Barcelona, works such as that of 1902, «*Crouching Woman*» (C.B. Nathhorst collection, Stockholm), «*La sopa*» («The Soup», Ontario Art Gallery, Canada), other paintings from the blue period, and the graceful and excellent watercolour, «*Blind Man's Meal*» (Gertrude Stein collection).

Here, the most adequate commentary comes from a woman who was intimately related to the artist, his first lover, Fernande Olivier. In her memoirs, published many years later, she remembered the disturbing effect that the discovery of Picasso's work caused, and particularly, the sight of a poor, gaunt and miserable man whose «stare reflected a sad resignation». And she asked: «what was at the bottom of all of it? Did it reveal a profound and desperate love of humanity, as I believed then, or was it a work of a cold mind as I have believed since?»

6

Knowing smiles appeared on the faces of the male residents of the house at No. 19 Ravignan Street in Montmartre, on the day in 1905 in which the rumour spread that an attractive model by the name of Fernande Olivier, resident of the same house, had moved in with her new friend, Pablo Picasso.

Some joker had nicknamed the house Bateau-Lavoir (literally, wash ship) because the shape of the building, largely built of wood, simulated the ships that were equipped as public washrooms on the River Seine. It was inhabited by laundresses, dressmakers, second hand merchants, actors, actresses, circus comics, literary men, writers, painters and aspiring painters, French, Germans and others. It was an environment of young, good-natured, sexually promiscuous and penniless people. Some aspired to glory. Others just wanted a place in the sun.

When she met Picasso, Fernande Olivier was already in great demand. Of the same age as the artist, with a strong build, strong hands and full face she was very lively with an intelligent and kind expression.

The professional models that the drawing schools

provided, in Paris as well as in Barcelona, were typically woman who posed nude as well as they could, with an inexpressive face and who abstained from flirting and under no circumstances would accept sexual requests from men.

Outside the schools, on the other hand, in the bohemian workshops, anything was possible. Some young women had decided to become models after difficult times, after being abandoned by their husbands or having abandoned them, as was the case of Fernande. Quite unlike other professional models, they were generally beautiful but little educated women, who were limited to posing as statues but Fernande, who had an artistic sensibility, also drew and painted. A self portrait that she kept of herself shows a sweet and expectant character. Next to Picasso, in photographs of the time, the girl appears a little taller than her companion, something that happened often to Picasso.

She was not really called Fernande nor Olivier, but Amélie Lang, as she herself explained in her *Souvenirs intimes*, published after her death, «I was the unwanted child of a single mother and a married and unknown father». This fact combined with a difficult upbringing explains why she wanted to start a new life and erase the past, presenting herself with a new name. It was not an original initiative. In the wild, bohemian, cosmopolitan city of Paris, whether out of snobbishness or for other reasons, it was not unusual for people to call themselves by pseudonyms. Wilhelm Apollinaris Kostrowitzky, of

Italian, Polish and German origins, named himself Guillaume Apollinaire, and it was with this name that he introduced himself to Picasso in 1905, with whom he shared a great friendship. Pierre Mac Orlan was the worker, poet and painter Pierre Dumarchey's pen name. Francesco Carcopino-Tusoli was the novelist of the slums who signed Francis Carco. And so on.

Fernande Olivier's affair with the Andalusian artist started in an idyllic manner. Elizabeth Cowling, art professor at Edinburgh University and author of a monograph about Picasso, explains that he, who was so distant from social conventionalisms but so proud of his partner, formally introduced Fernande to his parents in Barcelona in 1906 as his fiancée, as was the custom then, both in the middle class as well as the working class, who were precisely those that were allergic to the bohemian life.

»Picasso was short in stature, dark haired, chubby, anxious and disturbing», Fernande wrote in her memoirs. «He had dark, deep, strange, penetrating eyes, with an almost fixed stare. He had clumsy gestures and feminine hands, and was badly dressed and untidy. A shiny black lock of hair cuts across his intelligent forehead. Half bohemian, half worker in the way he dressed, his hair, that was too long, would brush the neck of his jaded jacket. We lived in the same house and we met each other all the time. During that time, it seemed that he was always out, at the Montmartre square, and I always asked myself, «when does this man work?» until I found

43

Fernande Olivier at about 1907-1908

out that he preferred painting at night so as not to be
bothered. During the day, in his room, there was a con-
tinuous procession of Spaniards (referring to the Catalonians that came from Barcelona)...One day he invited
me to enter his workshop; I was completely surprised
when I saw Picasso's work. Surprised and attracted. Its
morbid aspect somewhat bothered me, but it also fascinated me. Huge unfinished canvases decorated the
workshop, where everything breathed work. But what
an untidy mess, *grand Dieu!*»

Even so, it would not be her who did the washing up,
say some of those who met her and present her as lazy.
Elegant, sweet and a little naive, she could have con-
quered a prince. Fate, however, had brought her to this
burrow where, in the evenings one could smell the

saucepan which boiled (and this only on the days when the artist had earned something), mixed with the strong smell of paints and the heavenly smoke of prohibited opium.

The artist's work shocked all his acquaintances. Carles Junyer-Vidal, a Catalonian art critic and collector, had published in 1904 in the Madrid news paper *El Liberal* an article that began as follows: «Pablo Ruiz Picasso! Here is a man that for many is less than well-known and even those that know him, do not know him well enough to understand and judge him».

However there were some buyers that were capable of understanding Picasso's ever-changing work or, at least, of interpreting it in their own way. Such was the case of the North American Gertrude Stein, a woman of masculine features from a multimillionaire family of Jewish origin from Pennsylvania. Settled in Paris with her brother Leo, she wrote novels in English, served as patron of the arts, and appreciated Picasso's paintings, about whom she wrote a fictional book, but with some clairvoyant observations. Stein bought a handful of Picasso's paintings that allowed him to subsist for some time, after a period of misery.

»The first painting we bought from him», Stein explained, «was *Chica con cesta de flores'* («Girl with basket of flowers», Stein Collection, United States), elegant, classic and enchanting». A young lady in profile, nude and painted in the realist style, with the prevailing colour pink, a colour which at the time was dominant in Picasso's paintings of the circus, acrobats, jugglers and Amazons. «In 1905 he painted my portrait at the home of the dealer Sagot», the American patron of the arts recalls. «I posed for Picasso in some eighty sessions during the winter. He finally painted just the head, said that he could not look at me any longer and went to Spain. When he returned he finished the head without seeing me again and gave me the painting». The portrait (G. Stein's legacy, The Metropolitan Museum of Art, New York), in dark and reddish tones, depicts a bulky seated woman, with a thin nose, scornful stare and with one eye much bigger than the other. The explanation that the Picasso expert, J. Palau i Fabre, offers is that the artist «tried to make the face into a mask». However, the peculiar Mrs. Stein said: «I liked the painting, it is me and it is the only portrait that has been painted of me where I am always me.»

In 1905, Picasso invited a sullen youth from Montmartre, not yet 20 and with a reputation as one town thief, to model for him. The oil on canvas, 100 x 81 cm, *Garçon à la pipe* («Boy with Pipe»), (acquired at auction by an unknown buyer in New York in May 2004, for nearly $100 million) depicts the boy, dressed in dark blue overalls, sitting on a stool. The boy is holding a pipe to his heart with his left hand in a manner which looks somewhat artificial and his head is decorated with a crown of pink flowers. The back wall is, in this work, and probably for the last time, also painted with roses.

The boy's face is represented in a realist manner, but

his arms are elongated, in the style of El Greco, a fact that makes us think, as has been suggested in the case of Domenico Theotokópoulos, that Picasso might also have had a sight defect.

Among the rich eccentrics who passed through Picasso's workshop, to have a look or buy some pieces, there was one that invited him to spend some time on the coast of Holland, not far from Amsterdam, in June 1905. He returned with some drawings, one of which reveals new facets in the artist's life; this is *Barca en un Canal* («Boat on a canal», Musée Picasso, Paris). It's a very simple sketch in aquarelle with pink tones and, without a doubt, done very quickly. The subjects are only suggested by a silhouette and few lines more: two women with one child in the foreground, an anchored boat in the middle ground, and a typical windmill in the background. The composition is poor but of great softness and it manifests the already well known ability of Picasso to quickly sketch, whenever he pleased, a lively scene with four lines and some touches of colour. Did he draw it from real life? We do not know. It seems more likely that he based it on a work that he had seen in a museum. One could think that he had seen Rembrandts etching «*Omval*» in which can be seen, in the right foreground, a human figure, in the middle a boat, and in the background, a windmill.

Despite the patronage of the North Americans, Picasso only began to relax when, at the beginning of 1906, the collector and gallery owner Vollard bought a large number of his paintings. «The huge sum received by Picasso» writes Hélène Klein, curator of the Picasso Museum in Paris «allowed him to travel to Spain, passing through Barcelona to introduce his beautiful fiancée to his parents, and stay for over two months in Gósol, a village in upper Catalonia, where his work went through a decisive evolution that led him to the painting of *Demoiselles d'Avignon*, and from there to Cubism».

Fernande Olivier said that the time that they spent together in the Catalonian village was enchantingly wonderful. «In Paris, Picasso always seemed disoriented, out of place. I have never known a foreigner less apt for Paris than him», the French woman said. «On the other hand, in Spain, he was another man; in Gósol he was more delicate, not as savage, more talkative, lively». Running away to the Catalonian Mountains, Picasso had experienced a momentary calm. But where can one flee from the inexorable destiny that pursues him?

7

The Gósol village at a height of 1420m, on a plain behind the Pedraforca mountain, bordering the Pyrenees of Catalonia, administered by Spain, at 30 km in a straight line from the French-Spanish border.

At the beginning of the 20th century, only very few pioneers had ventured into hiking and climbing, and just a few select spirits were drawn to these great open spaces. The Barcelonian sculptor Enric Casanovas i Roy was one of those spirits. An artist of great finesse, he had exhibited some figures at «Els Quatre Gats» in Barcelona, had stayed for periods in Paris and, knowing the good that visiting Ports de Beseit and Horta had done for Picasso, he suggested an excursion to the region of Pedraforca.

In May 1906, Picasso and Fernande arrived, tired, at the Gósol villa. The steam train, fed with coal, only reached the town of Ripoll. There, a stagecoach with four horses had taken them to within sight of the Pyrenees along a small road. The last bit had to be done by mule, through the woods.

Workers, cattle-raisers, shepherds and smugglers,

nearly 700 souls populated the area of Gósol. The remains of the millennial castle, built as defence against the Muslim invasion, and the sharply pointed bell tower of the gothic church stood out against the smaller buildings, but the real centre of the village was the hostel «Cal Tempanada», a place which provided food, a boarding house, shelter for forest workers and travellers, a den for card players and, possibly a meeting place for *paquetaires*, in other words, the smugglers that came by foot across the border, with packages of products that the prohibition laws banned from entering freely. It was the only hoste in the town and was here that the beautiful French woman and the sullen Spaniard stayed.

Picasso was received with curiosity by the villagers who, in the tradition of small towns where everyone had a nickname, was rapidly given one, becoming after the first few weeks «Pau de Gósol» (Pau being the Catalonian version of Pablo).

The owner of the hostel, ex-smuggler Josep Fontdevila , 90 years of age, was a perfect example of the men of the region. «A ferocious old man, with a strange and savage beauty, who still, in spite of his age, had all his hair and teeth. Malicious and rude to everyone, he only showed a sense of humour with Picasso», Fernande wrote in her diary. The painter drew the former smuggler repeatedly, and one of these drawings, if it has not been lost, still hangs on a wall in the hostel.

There are few drawings and paintings which depict the villagepeople: a watercolour of a young man with a hat, the pleasing oil painting of the woman who sold bread (The Philadelphia Museum of Art), and little more. Picasso painted a far off view of the village's houses, but nature, the splendid landscapes of the region and the views of the sky are all missing in the series of paintings he did there. Though he liked to hunt and trek through the mountains, where the spirit had space to expand freely, the human figures he depicted are in small, claustrophobic environments, where it appears that the light of day has never entered.

This is certainly the impression given by two nudes painted in Gósol, *La toilette* (Albright Knox Art Gallery. Buffalo, USA) and *Grand nu debout* («Standing Nude», Mr. and Mrs. W. Paley collection, New York), using Fernande as a model. The first depicts the calm beauty of the model. In the second, the face's enigmatic grace is apparent. In both, the colours are warm, but the expressions seem stern, like the mute archaic Greek statues, and one could imagine that the young melancholy Picasso was becoming bored of painting this type of image and in a state of mind in contrast to that of the old Pierre Auguste Renoir. The uninhibited painter from the south of France, who painted bathers happily posing, continued setting up his easel on luxurious beaches at the age of 65 and had once said: «Ça ne m'amuse pas autant que de peindre unes fesse» (There is nothing that I like more than painting a bottom).

In contrast to Fernande's idyllic memories of Gósol, another painting that Picasso did of her causes surprise;

Fernande avec le mouchoir à la tête («Fernande with a scarf around her head», T.C. Jones, Virginia Museum of Fine Arts collection, USA). It looked nothing like her. Fernande had an oval face, rounded cheeks, a fine nose and a sensual mouth. The painting that the artist did of her depicts a woman with a long face, a twisted nose and tight, dry lips. The explanation? J. Palau i Fabre, a constant admirer of the painter, says that in Gósol Picasso « searched for diverse solutions to the problem of artistic expression...» and that finally, he decided to «ridicule the cult of feminine beauty, destroying it». How and why he reached this strange conclusion is not explained. All that one can think is that the boiling thoughts within the artist were about to explode with an uncontrolled force.

8

«A nervous fear of illnesses caused Picasso to leave Gósol. The cleaning lady at the hostel had come down with typhus and Picasso wanted to leave quickly and return directly to France», Fernande wrote. «The mountain region was only accessible by mule. It was therefore necessary to cross the Pyrenees. I remember leaving Gósol at five o'clock in the morning and arriving at five o'clock in the afternoon at a village where we took a stagecoach».

When the couple finally returned to Paris, Picasso shut himself in to prepare some sketches for a painting for which he had already thought of a title: «Le salaire du péché» («The wages of sin»). The imaginary scene was a whorehouse. In the corner one can see the figure of a smiling sailor, and on the other side, a medical student who has entered the room with a skull in hand, a reference to death caused by syphilis and other venereal diseases.

Unhappy with the results, Picasso worked on other, different sketches. The sailor and the student were erased and in their place, feminine figures appeared, the residents of the house. The artist now wanted to call it: «Le Bordel d'Avignon» («The brothel of Avignon), making reference to a whorehouse that he knew on Avinyó Street in Barcelona. However, his friend, Max Jacob, who had taken him in when he first arrived in Paris and had taught him the basics of the French language, convinced Picasso to forget this title which referred to a «house of pleasure» and to elevate the status of these professionals by naming them «ladies».

The definitive title *Les demoiselles d'Avignon* was chosen and as the French were unsurprisingly unaware of the existence of a street of this name in Barcelona, they believed that it referred to Avignon in Provence, the famous city where the popes from the Middle Ages resided.

At this time, Picasso, through his friendship with Apollinaire, met Georges Braque, a Normandy native who was a year younger than him, a former apprentice of a wall painter, who had decided he wanted to do artistic painting. Braque and Picasso worked together, and together they followed the same obsession: to do something which had never before been done in painting.

After a number of preparatory sketches, Picasso painted five full female bodies of women with Guinyolesque characteristics, set in a place without perspective. Two of the women appear to be wearing masks, similar to certain African masks and stone statues from the Iberian archaic period that, gifts from friends or the emissary of Apollinaire, he kept in his studio. Two of the remaining women stare out at the viewer with masked eyes and a mischievous expression. Their noses are drawn in profile and their lips are just a suggestion represented by a line. The fifth figure sits on a stool with her back to the viewer, but the face looks forward with a crooked mouth. A hand, apparently belonging to no-one, extends from a head at the top of the painting. At the bottom is a piece of watermelon next to a handful of grapes, and the spaces between the figures are filled with a convulsed magma that may not have any meaning.

«Picasso painted the *Les demoiselles d'Avignon* slowly,» said Gertrude Stein «and the final result was frightening. I remember that Txukin, the Russian collector and admirer of Picasso's work, came to my home after having seen the painting and said to me, almost in tears, «what a loss for French art!»

Braque was also horrified as Robert Hughes, the feared contemporary art critic from New York describes: «Braque was appalled by the ugliness and intensity of the painting...The women, more than prostitutes, appeared to be judges».

And J. Palau i Fabre certifies: «All the artist's friends disapproved of his venture..., only one man understood the artist: the dealer and critic D.H. Kahnweiler».

This unique man, Daniel-Henry Kahnweiler, was a Jewish German, 23 years old, who, as soon as he arrived in Paris in 1907, opened an art gallery. Without any artistic experience, but as keen as hawk in business, he sensed that the brutal expressionism, which from the beginning of the century had begun to make a mark in Germany, was a sign of new times and that in Paris, the capital of novelty, all that was new would become fashionable and all that was fashionable would sell well.

Picasso, discouraged by the fact that only the introverted and cerebral young German approved of his *Les demoiselles d'Avignon,* took it down from the wall and put it in a corner of the workshop from where it would not emerge for many years.

The personal frustration of the artist must have been considerable but, from a distance, R. Hughes says that «Picasso was then so little known, and Braque completely unknown, that neither of the two really existed as an artist in the public sphere (...). The group of friends that enjoyed their work was no more than a dozen people, formed by other painters, their lovers, the dark German dealer, Daniel-Henry Kahnweiler, and themselves, who were in constant praise of each other.»

In spite of this uneasiness, Braque and Picasso continued painting together, in quest of their impossible aim like the alchemists of the Middle Ages, who had tried in vain to find a way to turn metals like lead into gold. It was a quest which the expert André Fermigier describes as «a very mysterious adventure, which marked a rupture with all the traditions of the art of painting».

9

«Maybe it was the opium that allowed me to understand the true meaning of the word love», wrote Fernande Olivier in her diary. And it is also her who describes the hair-raising events of the house at No. 19 Ravignan Street, where, one day in June 1908, Wiegels, a German painter who lived in the house, hung himself from a beam in his studio after a night of excessive opium taking.

Picasso was so frightened of death that he never again used the drug which guaranteed an ephemeral trip to an artificial paradise, but without a secured return ticket. From then on, he contented himself with the temporary euphoria incited by hash, the sweet aroma that filled the «Cabaret of the Assassins» when it was smoked, but which could also be taken in the form of a pill.

The Cabaret of the Assassins was an old Montmartre bar, with macabre paintings and objects on the walls. One painting represented a madman slitting the throat of his own family, and a knife, supposedly stained with blood, was hung to one side. The place was really called

Lapin à Gill (Rabbit of Gill) ever since it had been taken over by a Mr Gill and later changed to *Le Lapin agile* (The Agile Rabbit), but everyone knew it by its old name. It was not the only place in Montmartre with a suspicious name. «Many bars names were obscene, true brothels, hidden drunkenness, orgies, rape, crimes...» wrote the Catalan, Ferran Canyameras, who as writer, business man and patron of the bohemian artists knew Paris well.

In the beginning, «The Cabaret» was a place visited solely by rogues, tramps, whores and the curious. But as Montmartre became known as a centre for artists, it had become a meeting place for cosmopolitan bohemians, painters, sculptures and writers with their respective, or shared, friends, and was visited by rich tourists with mundane lives, curious about the environment or interested in the art.

For Picasso, Wiegels suicide reminded him of Casagemas' suicide, the Catalonian friend with whom with he had travelled for the first time in France, as well as the death of his sister Concepción, who died at seven years of age when he was only 14. Death instilled an extreme fear in him, and to get rid of it, he spent a month in a country house surrounded by forest, near to the isolated village of La Rue-des-Bois not far from Paris.

Landscapes were not his favourite thing, but he returned to Paris with canvases inspired by landscapes, though deformed by strong shapes and geometrical forms that hinted at what would soon be called «cubism».

Picasso continued unknown to the general public, but the praise he was given by art critics, who were often also collectors such as Apollinaire, the American Gertrude Stein, the German Wulhem Uhde and others, increased sales of his work. They were good times to buy works that did not resemble classical paintings. France was at the time experiencing what would later be called the *Belle Époque,* and the Bourgeoisie believed, as did Virgil of Imperial Rome, that Paris, France, and its Belle Epoque were eternal. Picasso, infected with the economic euphoria of the dealers and collectors and now free from money worries, accustomed himself to spending the summer in places far from Paris. He had a preference for Catalonia but spent time in both the French and the Spanish territories; Horta de Sant Joan and Cadaqués (Spanish Catalonia), and Ceret, on the border of Perpignan (French Catalonia).

There was peace in Europe. World powers were in angry dispute over territories and borders and the alliances made one day might be broken the next, but the tensions were hidden by diplomatic abilities that, with a velvet glove, covered the iron fist. Meanwhile, protected by a predominating tolerance, the «à la page» intellectuals encouraged irrational ideas in a field that was apparently as unknown as the arts. On February 22nd 1909, the Italian writer, F.T. Marinetti published the Futurist Manifesto in the Parisian news paper, Le Figaro, the mouthpiece of the bourgeoisie. «Nothing that does not have an aggressive character can be a work of art..., we want to glorify war once more...we want to destroy museums, libraries and academies» Marinetti wrote, and maybe many readers preferred to think of the text as the provocation of writers and artists, who, already known as peculiar people, were inoffensive even if the critics labelled them as mad.

There was peace in Europe if the break between the two world wars can be seen as such. In Horta de St Joan, isolated from the rest of the world, a supreme sense of calm reigned. Picasso, having visited the place as a child, returned there in 1909 with his fiancée Fernande. However, the second time is never as good as the first and although the old people of the village with whom Picasso had spent time years before received him with open arms, the village gossips were scandalized by the fact that he was living with his partner out of wedlock.

The fact that the couple met at night in the town bar to drink and play cards or dominoes with local men accompanied by a guitar, the only instrument that Picasso liked, until the early hours did not add to the positive picture. According to the erudite J. Palau i Fabre, many years after the visit people still remembered two women who had thrown rocks at the windows of the hostel where Picasso and Fernande were staying and that he «came out on the balcony yelling and threatening them with a gun». Fernande, in her memoirs, said that the gun «was a Browning that Picasso always had on him. He had this bad habit» and she adds that, in Montmartre, «returning at night with their friends, often drunk, singing or yelling, he would wake up the neighbourhood with gunshots».

While these incidents were occurring, the work that Picasso painted in his second and last stay in Horta de Sant Joan, are highly valued by museums and collectors. *La Bassa d'Horta* («The Horta Pond», Private collection, Paris), *La Fàbrica d'Horta* («The Horta Factory», Hermitage Museum, St. Petersburg, Russia) and a portrait of Fernande (Kunstammlung Nordheim-Westfalen. Düsseldorf, Germany) stand out.

The last painting was strangely executed. Certainly, Fernande would not have liked to hang it on the dining room wall, in the hypothetical case that her lover had given it to her. This is not a negative criticism. J. Palau i Fabre, the devout and constant admirer of Picasso, says of this portrait: «The beautiful Fernande is submitted to the rhythm of the composition, causing one to forget that it is of a beautiful woman at all.» Is this one of the mysteries of «Cubism»?

At the height of summer, while the youths Fernande and Picasso spent their time in Horta de Sant Joan, the city of Barcelona, where the artist's parents lived, trembled with fear and hatred.

A people's revolt against the terrible working conditions and against the mobilization of soldiers for the Moroccan war, had unpredictably turned into a religious pursuit with scenes of medieval horror. In the week between the end of July and August 2nd 1909, in a Barcelona that was given over to the incendiary agita-

61

tors, eighty religious buildings, churches, chapels and convents were burnt. Three priests were murdered. Embalmed nuns were sacked from their tombs, dragged along the smouldering streets and left on the corners to be mocked.

The impact of the so called «Tragic Week» was deeply felt in Barcelona society, and among those who suffered serious emotional injury were the parents of Picasso. The health of his father, Sr José Ruiz, an orderly and sensitive man, worsened. He was already a man disillusioned by life, disillusioned by the path taken by his son the painter and hurt by the scarce affection he was shown by this son. His mother, Sra María Picasso, had already guessed that Pablo's wedding with his kind French «fiancée» would be postponed ad calendas graecas.

In autumn 1909, Pablo Picasso announced to the family that he was moving to a different home. He was

The factory of Horta. Horta 1909

going to live in an elegant and well lit flat on the Boule-vard Clichy. The only problem, as Fernande pointed out, was that they did not have any furniture. His father, who already was 71 years old, collected together all of the old furniture that he had in Barcelona and sent it to the new residence of his boy in Paris. Was this, perhaps, the last time that he would help him?

10

Among the scholars of art history there is general agreement that attributes the initiation of «Cubism» to Paul Cézanne. This middle-class artist from Aix-en-Provence, painter of portraits, landscapes and still lives, did not receive official recognition from the great and the good of Paris until, at the age of 56, the art dealer Vollard organized an exhibition of his work in the French capital.

Cézanne was a man full of doubts that sought an original road, trying out works which were far from the notions of classical perspective and the formal harmony. There is great disagreement in the large number of writings about the artist. In the run up to the twenties, Walter Sickert, the most important English impressionist painter and art critic, labelled his work as «deplorable and shameful», and added, in another context, that «Picasso was a feeble caricature of the failures of Cézanne». Subsequently, in 1972, the Catalan critic D. Giralt Miracle wrote that «Cézanne contributed to painting a true dignity and value».

Despite this, «Cubism» is normally considered the

invention of Picasso and Braque. It is also generally accepted that the cubist style tries to give a complete picture of the object(s) depicted, as if the viewer could see from all perspectives. In other words, that it did not try to represent reality as the common mortal saw it, but to «present» an abstract personal idea —or an accumulation of ideas and sensations— by means of forms that are nonexistent in nature.

Regarding the origin of the word «Cubism», some say that it was the painter Matisse who invented it when he was surprised by the sight of a number of cubist forms in the paintings of Braque. Others like H. Klein, director of the Picasso Museum in Paris, maintain that «the responsibility for the word Cubism is attributed to the art critic L. Vauxcelles, for having evoked the reduction of forms to cubes in the paintings exhibited by Braque at the Kahnweiler gallery in 1908».

Whether Vauxcelles used the word seriously to describe the new style or whether he did it ironically, we do not know. In any case, Fernande Olivier, Picasso's lover, remarks in her memoirs that «later, Vauxcelles, in a state of irritation, declared that the artists were no more than Cubist «patagons». Literally, a patagon is, in French, a person pertaining to the native population of the Patagònia, a rough region of the southern extreme of America. But in the context of such phrase, and in the colloquial French of the time, that of the colonization by Europeans from far off territories, patagon had a scornful meaning, suggesting a primitive and ignorant person.

The line that Picasso persisted in following was causing him to lose some of his original admirers, for example, the counsellor of the French State Olivier Sainsère and the Russian collector Txukin. But others, like the art dealers Vollard and Kahnweiler, continued buying his works without fail, at the same time as they opened up the road of social ascent.

The Pitxots, a powerful family from Barcelona established in Empordà, a region of the Spanish Catalonia, on the frontier with the French Catalonia, were interested in Picasso. The Pitxots are considered the «discoverers», towards the end of the 19th century, of Cadaqués, an isolated fishing town, closed in by the mountains and the sea that, since the mid 20th century, has become a fashionable tourist centre due to the fame given to it by the painter S. Dali. As the story goes, Ramon Pitxot, ten years older than Picasso, and also a painter, had a splendid house in Cadaqués and invited the Malagan painter to visit in the summer of 1910. They had previously exhibited together in Paris, and the Malagan accepted the invitation. However, both shared a bad dream. It was because of frustrated love for Ramon Pitxot's wife that the troubled Casagemas, Picasso's companion on his first trip to Paris, had killed himself.

In the decade of the eighties of the 19th century, the extraordinary painter, a landscape artist from Barcelona, Eliseu Meifrén, had been one of the first artists to paint the wild, attractive coast of Cadaqués. Her «*marines*» are today highly sought after by art collectors. For Picasso, on the other hand, the landscapes left him indifferent. «More than stopping to confront the landscape, Picasso had to face, above all, himself», says J. Palau i Fabre, who also says that his paintings of Cadaqués «represent the achievement of pure abstraction», an example of which is the oil on canvas *Le Guitarriste* («The Guitarist», Musée National d'Art Moderne. Paris).

What person Picasso would have to face, a few months later, was the French Police. The issue was a delicate one.

In 1911, accompanied by Fernande Olivier, Picasso had spent a relaxed summer in Ceret (French Catalonia). But when he returned to Paris, his intimate friend and propagandist, Apollinaire, worriedly passed on the news to him that *The Gioconda* by Leonardo Da Vinci had been stolen from the Louvre. The police were connecting the robbery to a previous one which had taken place five years earlier and in which some Iberian masks and sculptures had been stolen. Some of these were the very same ones given to Picasso by Apollinaire's emissary to keep hidden. In consequence both Apollinaire and Picasso had been ordered to present themselves for a court hearing.

H. Klein, the curator of the Picasso Museum of Paris, says: «Towards the end of May 1911, an individual returned to the newspaper *Paris-Journal*, on the condition of anonymity, an Iberian sculpture that he himself claimed to have stolen from the Louvre. He added that in March 1907 he had stolen two more that he had left in the care of a Parisian painter (Picasso)! The thief identified himself as Géry Pieret, and his connections with Apollinaire, also suspect in the theft of *The Gioconda*, resulted in Apollinaire spending five days in Santé Prison. The presence of those two heads carved in stone, beautiful pieces of Iberian art from the 3rd century BC, at Picasso's workshop, in 1907, is of essential importance in the stylistic evolution of the painter, which was then to be seen in full flower in the *Demoiselles d'Avignon*.»

A passive but direct witness of the facts, Fernande Olivier explained that the thief, «son of a good family, intelligent and bohemian, possessor of a kind of madness which had pushed him to steal the statues and masks for sheer folly, to entertain by showing that it was easy to steal from the Louvre...Picasso was not accused, but he was asked to be at the disposal of the examining magistrate as witness...all in all, after a certain time, the matter was filed, but Picasso and Apollinaire believed for a long time that they continued to be watched...They had reacted like children».

The scare had left a bad memory in the tormented conscience of Picasso, to whom the following phrase is attributed: «I paint, as others write their biographies. My finished works are the pages of my diary.» In light of this statement, be it authentic or apocryphal, observing the painting *Bouteille of Vieux Marc* («Bottle of Old Marc», Musée National de Art Moderne. Paris) painted in Ceret in 1912, we can see that there is a page of a newspaper which is very revealing of Picasso's troubled thoughts. Under the title of the newspaper one can read the news: «*On arrête une artiste accussée d'empoisonner son amant*» « (Artist has been detained accused of poisoning his lover).

The association of ideas in the mind of Picasso seems evident.

Detention of an artist: Himself!

Wanting to be rid of his lover: Picasso was at the time flirting with another woman and was ready to leave Fernande.

In May 1912, Picasso threw Fernande out of his house on the pretext that she too had been flirting, we can ignore up to what point, with another painter. Certainly, Fernande did not leave with a painting by the artist under her arm. According to her friends, she walked out onto the street with eleven French Francs in her purse.

PART TWO

11

Ever since the sculptor Manolo M. Hugué had introduced him to the tranquil Pyrenean village of Ceret in the Vallespir region near Perpignan, 12 km from the French-Spanish border, Picasso had been returning there for the summer.

The population was less than 4,000 and the foreigners that visited were amateur students of historic monuments and the arts attracted by the typicality of the village which retained part of its 18th century walls. Some artists had also been seduced by the diaphanous light of the region, similar to that of Provence, and by the friendly landscape of chestnuts and oaks that grew on the outskirts. Like the rest of the population of the Vallespir and Rosselló region, Ceret had been under the control of the Catalonian-Aragonese confederation during the middle ages, and though in 1674 it came under French control, and towards the end of the 19th century, French had become obligatory in schools, the natives continued to speak Catalan and maintained Catalan traditions.

Among the artists that began to meet or live in Ceret, were the musician Déodat de Séverac, the sketcher and painter Martí Vives and the art patron and collector Frank Burty Haviland, with the aid of whom the sculptor Manolo M. Hugué had established himself there.

Manolo, as everyone called him, was son of a poor Barcelonian widow, Anna Hugué, and of a soldier named Martínez, who had deceived her with promises of marriage and then abandoned her at the same time refusing to recognise paternity of his son. The widow died shortly after the birth and Manolo had gone to live a drunken life in the slums of Barcelona, where, after working as a wax touch up worker in a forge, he began to sculpt figures that immediately caught the attention of art dealers, for example Kahnweiler, «the only man that had understood Picasso».

That season, Picasso had changed both lover and flat. The new maiden was the French woman Eva Gouel, whom the artist honoured in the oil painting *Le violon* («The Violin», Staatsgalerie, Sttutgart) that he painted in Ceret. On the picture the inscription «Jolie Eva» can be read. The expert Paula Izquierdo says that Eva was «a little bourgeoisie, sweet and delicate, willing to love one man only, to do it happily in exchange for protection» and that «together they went to Barcelona, where Picasso wanted to present her to his friends and parents as his future wife». Would he be successful in this second attempt at marriage? It would not take long to find out.

Favourable winds were blowing for the *avantguards*, a bellicose word signifying the first line of an army, which also came to be used to describe artistic subver-

74

sion, following in the steps of the futuristic Marinetti, clairvoyant writer of inflammatory prose and at the same time a convinced militarist. The pre-war environment contaminated the vocabulary of writers and art critics who were considered leaders of the art of the future. Apollinaire, for example, collaborated in the French magazine *La Phalange*, a Greek word signifying the «body of the Greek infantry», antiquity, and the fame of the invincible, although the magazine had nothing to do with the military. The young Italian artists who had signed the Manifesto of Futurist painting in 1910 did not preoccupy themselves with war strategy either but instead thought about painting. Nevertheless, the vocabulary of these rebellious texts is (perhaps naively) more suggestive of proclamations of war than those of artists: «With this enthusiastic adhesion to futurism, we aim to destroy the cult of the past...to exalt whatever form of originality although it may be reckless, although it may be violent...we want to rebel against the tyranny of the words HARMONY and GOOD TASTE...we want to represent real life, tumultuously transformed by victorious science. Let the dead people be buried in the deepest bowels of the land! Give way to youth, to the violent, to the reckless!»

The first to give way were the art dealers and certain art critics. In February 1912 an exhibition of the work of the futurists opened at the Bernheim-Jeune gallery in Paris, and Apollinaire extolled, in writing, the connections he saw between Futurism and Cubism. The two tendencies were not on exactly the same wavelength, but there were common interests and personal connections. Even Marinetti, founder of Futurism, had explicitly gone to Montmartre to speak to the Cubists. At the hotel where he stayed he was received at nightfall by Picasso and Apollinaire, who, with open mouths, endured an entire night listening to the inexhaustible but indisputably brilliant and terrible monologue of the Italian supporter of the glorification of war.

The price of fashionable paintings was rising day by day and some art dealers had to agree to the increasingly ardent economic demands of their artists. Picasso was among the favoured ones in this new economic prosperity, but he would have been wrong to believe that now he would be happier. The factor «if it were not for» blocked his path. If it were not for the fact that Eva, his new fiancée, had bad health. If it were not for the obligatory military service of three years in France which was like a horrible omen, if it were not for the fact that his father had little life left to live.

His father, Sr. José Ruiz Blasco, died on May 2nd, 1913, at 75 years of age, in his house at the end of Princess Street in Barcelona, leaving his widow, Sra María Picasso, and daughter Lola. Since they were a discreet family, few things are known about them, but the American Gertrude Stein, who had spoken to the family, gives us some idea: «The father seemed English. Tall, with red hair, he had an almost English form of imposing himself. The mother was from a family of silversmiths.

Physically, the mother was like Picasso. Small and strong, with an energetic body, dark skin, and medium fine, smooth black hair. Physically, Picasso resembles his mother, whose surname he adopted.»

Picasso was then 32 years old and it was during this phase of his life that his father came to be no longer idealized or respected, but instead seen as retrograde, a man that had made mistakes and, often, seen as the person responsible for Picasso's unhappiness. Since settling in Paris, the encounters between Picasso and his parents had been brief, according to the recollections of Fernande Olivier who says: «In Barcelona, Picasso had his family, but dedicated the least possible time to them.» Nor is there any certainty that he attended his father's funeral, celebrated in the Catalonian capital. The expert P. Izquierdo affirms that «he was not present». And it is known that the mourning of the son for the death of its father did not last very long. The month after the death, in June, Picasso returned to Ceret with Eva, and from there he went to Figueres (Empordà, Spanish Catalonia), according to J. Palau i Fabre, «to attend a course on bulls», his youthful fondness.

Life continued its unstoppable course and the imminence of a war between France and Germany did not worry everyone. The *furor teutonicus* exalted the spirits of the German youth in the same way that the chauvinists of *la France éternelle* inflamed a large part of French youth.

On June 28th 1914, the murder of the archduke of

Austria and his wife, allies of Germany, in Sarajevo, was the spark which ignited the European continent. On July 31st, an extreme socialist murdered Jean Jaurès, the founder of the French Socialist Party, for being opposed to the entry of France in the war against Germany. On August 2nd 1914 the war exploded, and it was as if, suddenly, time stopped. In Paris, the wind blew away the rapidly hung posters on the walls of the police precincts which gave notice of the order of the government: general mobilization of the armed forces! «In France, the soldiers went to the front very enthusiastically», says Alícia Marcet, lecturer at the University of Perpignan, «but here, in French Catalonia, they were even more so, due to the fact that the head of the French army was a native Catalan from Ribesaltes (Rosselló), general Joseph Joffre».

The explosion of the war caught Picasso and Eva Gouel on holidays in Avignon and surprised Kahnweiler in Italy, where he had gone on a business trip. Apolitical in temperament, the painter as well as the art dealer felt very out of place.

Since Picasso was a foreign resident in France, and citizen of the Spanish State that had been declared neutral, he would not be obliged to carry out military service, but he, who had always moved with the group, realized that many of his companions would be mobilized or dispersed and he that would remain practically alone with Eva, who was sick, in Paris.

The German Kahnweiler, who tried to return to

Eva Gouel

France where he had an art gallery full of paintings, found that, at the border, the police would not let him enter as he was a citizen of an enemy state and therefore a possible spy. If he returned to Germany he would be obliged to take up arms against the French, something he had no desire to do. Solution? He took refuge in Switzerland.

The Frenchman Georges Braque, naturally, was mobilized *ipso facto*.

Apollinaire, on the other hand, could have avoided going to the front, as, despite his French name he was not a French citizen. Son of an Italian man and Polish woman, he was born in Rome, and, in those initial moments of the conflict, Italy was neutral. But Apollinaire, who had declared himself a dedicated futurist, due to his idealism, eagerness for adventure or for whatever other reason, presented himself to the French authorities as a volunteer for the front and was admitted.

In 1915, Italy joined the war on the side of France and the other allies fighting against Germany and their allies and many futurist artists would end up badly wounded on the front.

In Paris the fun was over. The city spent the evenings in darkness to avoid attacks by the zeppelins, the German airborne craft that, loaded with bombs, patrolled the skies amongst the clouds.

Dancing was prohibited. Almost all the theatres and dancehalls were seized by the government and used as ammunition stores. The Moulin Rouge closed its doors with lock and key, and the owner of the place, Josep Oller, like the other rich people that could afford it, took refuge far from the capital, in a small rural village.

After their stay in Avignon, Picasso and Eva had returned to a Paris which was not the one they knew and the environment that the solitary couple breathed in their flat appeared the prelude to a Greek tragedy. Eva, who had to be operated on for cancer, was very weak. She entertained herself weaving balaclavas for the soldiers, but these were her final hours. And Picasso, whom nature had given a compulsive, insatiable sexual urge that, it appeared, neither reason nor will could counteract, sought the consolation of another woman. According to John Richardson, the faithful living biographer of Picasso, who has accumulated a huge amount of documentation about the artist, in a letter dated December 13th 1915, the art collector S. Ferat communicates to the futurist painter A. Soffici that «Eva is dying, but there has been another woman in Picasso's life for the last seven months». The other woman has been identified as the young Gaby Depeyre, a resident of the neighbourhood of Montparnasse who had worked as a dancer in a cabaret.

Eva Gouel, the «Jolie Eva», second «fiancée» of the Andalusian painter, died on a chilly day in the second year of the First World War, December 14th, 1915. In the house, coal was scarce for heating the stove and on the street the sirens of the ambulances that passed could be heard. The war front was only a few kilometres away and nurses and undertakers could not be spared. Only Picasso, Max Jacob and five other people attended her burial.

12

If Picasso had had a good counsellor nearby, and had listened to him, he would not have taken the wrong turns that he took after Eva's death. Firstly, he asked Gaby Depeyre, the cabaret dancer, to marry him, something she refused to do as she had another lover. Secondly and still worse, he asked the same question to Irene Lagut, a bisexual woman who, according to John Richardson who knows everything about Picasso, was «a young Russian without prejudice, who loved to dance until the early hours, was a fan of drinking and who liked women more than men. She personified, in many ways, the new type of girl that had arisen in the course of the war: Amoral, barefoot and reckless». They were lovers, it is said, for a year, but the Russian, with everything prepared for the wedding, had a rethink and decided not to go ahead.

In times of war, the comedies of the civil population, in a place far from the battle lines, were often episodes that could never have been imagined by those who experienced them. Persistent as Picasso was in his search for a wife, he lacked stimulus for painting, and in a city empty of happiness was obliged to find amusement. Max Jacob, his old friend, who had taught him his first words in French when he arrived in Paris, had made a transcendental decision and needed Picasso to help him. Five years older than the Malagan painter, Max Jacob was a Normandy native of a Jewish family, an imaginative, extravagant writer, enthusiastic painter, bohemian joker, particularly when under the influence of alcohol and drugs, an ascetic and in general a very good man with religious doubts. He had decided to abandon the religion of Moses with which he had been brought up, and that he did not practice, and convert to Christianity. In taking the step he needed someone to act as godfather at the baptism. Since his circle of friends had been scattered by the war, he had no other option than to choose Picasso to be the godfather and witness to the conversion, despite the fact that he was allergic to priests.

In the streets, in front of provision shops, long queues of women and of men formed, and people gathered at the improvised blood donation centres.

It was not the best time to hold exhibitions, there were no spaces left open in which to do it, no public interested in visiting them, but, to entertain himself, Paul Poiret, a couturier of high fashion, invited half a dozen of artists, Picasso among them, to exhibit works in the luxurious parlour of his store near the Champs-Élysées. Taking advantage of the opportunity, Picasso decided to show, for the first time, the canvas that he had kept at the bottom of a cabinet for years and which had been praised by only one person: *Les Demoiselles d'Avignon.*

Despite the impression that the picture caused on guests of the couturier, Picasso got the chance to meet people from Parisian high society who could open doors for him within the slow but gradual social ascent that he was already experiencing. A reinforcement in this direction came to him, in a unexpected way, in the form of Jean Cocteau, 28 years old and a scandalous, morbid figure, born in a majestic castle, property of his family, near the forest of Fontainebleau. At the beginning of the war, he had helped the injured in an ambulance, but his homosexuality went against him: the military authorities considered that he had socialised in too friendly a manner with some young sailors and he was arrested. Having carried out his punishment and after returning to civil life and good company, he wrote a script for a ballet titled *Parade*, and proposed that Picasso design and paint the scenery and costumes. The show, with music by the modernist Eric Satie, was performed by the dancers of the Russian company of Serge Diaghilev, which was then on tour throughout Europe having previously toured America.

Both Satie and Diaghilev were famous and despite the official restrictions imposed due to the war, the Théâtre du Châtelet was able to open its doors to the public on May 18th 1917 for the ballet. The premiere was a public failure and a scandal. The public felt offended and mocked by the noises of aeroplane engines and typewriter keyboards which Satie had included and confused by the paintings of Picasso which varied from the realist opening scene to the Cubist costumes. As M. McCully points out, the performance was considered an intent to mock French culture, at a time when French patriots' susceptibility had risen to dangerous heights. But, if it was a matter of «épater the bourgeoisie», then the event can perhaps be considered as a «scandalous success», as H. Klein, curator of the Picasso Museum of Paris, has said.

The reception of the Russian ballerinas in Barcelona was very different. On November 10th of the same year, 1917, the show was premiered at the *Gran Teatre del Liceu* in the Catalonian capital. «The success was so great that they had to keep coming back», writes the reputable music critic Roger Alier.

Picasso, who followed the troup of the Russian ballerinas, also went to Barcelona, accompanied by a dancer with a stylised body. Her name was Olga Koklova and she appeared to be Picasso's new «fiancée».

PART THREE

13

With the departure from Barcelona of Diaghilev's Russian ballerinas, Picasso, accompanied by the dancer Olga Koklova, prolonged his stay in the city where, once the dead resulting from the recent local fight between labourers and police were buried, the middle-class could return without fear to the Liceu.

In Barcelona the people were occupied by the opera, cafe-concerts, silent movies, popular dances and football, the supporters of Catalonian autonomy had been appeased by having obtained a certain amount of regional power, and also by the security that, however long the war lasted, Spain would remain neutral.

Sra María, Picasso's mother, who still was mourning the death of her husband, hoped to be able to meet her son on this occasion and her wishes came true. She wasn't surprised when Pablo introduced Olga as his new «fiancée», but later, speaking alone with the young dancer, Sra María, moved by the bittersweet feelings of motherhood, told her: «Poor girl! You do not know what you are getting yourself into. I doubt that my son will ever make any woman happy.»

It is probable that her words were not exactly these. The biographers were not present. However, the general sentiment is taken as a true record and without doubt corresponds to reality. At least this is how Françoise Gilot, author of four books on Picasso, whom she met in the forties and with whom she formed a later friendship, reports it.

Olga Koklova, ten years younger than Picasso, was born in Ukraine, the nation that separates Romania from Russia, where the Bolshevik revolution had taken place. It has not been proved that the dancer was the daughter of a colonel in a noble family, as has been said, but it does not matter. The photographic portraits that are kept of her show an elegant girl, and her granddaughter Marina, in the book *Grand-père*, presents her as a long suffering and responsible woman.

Being in Barcelona, Picasso portrayed his new conquest in an oil painting, *Olga amb mantellina* (Olga with Cloak»), a highly realistic painting. In the canvas, Olga is depicted as a rural youth, wearing a traditional festival dress from her country; a woman with a clear face, ample cheekbones, tight lips and the powerful chin of a strong woman who knows how to instil respect.

There are few doubts about the strong character of Koklova. Otherwise, she would not have obliged Picasso to get married in an orthodox Christian ritual at the orthodox church in Paris, when the Great War was barely over, after having been married by civil procedure at the town hall on July 12th 1918. Picasso's great friends acted as witnesses: Max Jacob, Apollinaire, with his head bandaged because of a shrapnel injury, and Jean Cocteau. Picasso's magnetic looks had attracted many women and had dominated them, but the Ukrainian was made of harder stuff and it appears that the marriage between the two was a marriage of convenience, a marriage of adults, of those that seek solid companionship, without the expectation of «real love».

The dispersion of his friends during the war had converted Picasso into as solitary a man as Robinson on the desert island and his repeated failures to marry had pushed him to seek, with impatience, a stable partner.

Olga, with her background as a travelling artist, and having experienced the tiring work of ballet tours throughout the Americas and Europe, was aware that she would never achieve the category of prima ballerina and that she would never be able to return to her country, which was desperately fighting off the invasion of its old enemy, Russia. Olga was one of the many exiles in Paris that came from Eastern countries under Russian influence. The immense country with the its freezing steppes, in the hands of the Bolsheviks, would end up over running the Ukraine and persecuting the middle-classes or those considered as such with the confiscation of goods, famine or arms.

Olga, however, knew that she was surrounded by the international fame of the Diaghilev Ballet. She had met princes, princesses and the bourgeoisie and had developed good relations with influential people. In this sense she was, therefore, a good catch for Picasso. And ever since the moment that Diaghilev had considered him an artist with promise, it had seemed to her that this good catch was mutual.

A flat on la Boétie Street, which runs from the Boulevard Malesherbes to the luxurious avenue of the Champs Élysées, became the home of the love-nest which accorded to the social condition of the newly-weds in being properly attended by a maid, a cook and a driver.

Just as the war ended, and the dead, the injured and the unknown soldiers were counted, Europe was overcome by the influenza epidemic. Apollinaire would be one of its victims. But at the Napoleonic Arc de Triomphe in the Place de l'Étoile, where the Champs Élysées began, the red, white and blue flag of the French Republic flew victoriously, accompanied by the deep sounds of «The Marseilleise». And while sculptors in France were called upon to erect monuments to the *Morts pour la Patrie*, in the Paris of the Champs Élysées the champagne flowed once more as it had in the heady and distant times of the «Belle Époque». Peace reigned and nothing mattered.

The end of the conflict allowed Ambroise Vollard, the Parisian art dealer with his infallible instinct, to sell a large quantity of paintings which he had stored in a narrow store on Lafitte Street and to move to a splendid mansion on Martignac Street, which also served as an art gallery. He also bought two stately houses on the outskirts: one near Versailles and the other near the famous forest of Fontainebleau.

The German Kahnweiler did not have the same luck. His entire collection of pictures, which he had stored in his Paris gallery, was seized by the French State as «goods of the enemy». The German eagle had been brought down and lay, badly wounded, on the battlefield, surrounded by clay and the blood of the innocent. In the resulting climate of increasing mutual hatred between the French and Germans, Kahnweiler could not be forgiven.

In the case of Sergei Txukin, the rich Russian collector, the fifty of works by Picasso that he had stored in Moscow were seized by the Bolsheviks. Despite this, he managed to save his own skin and took refuge in Paris.

Thanks to Olga Koklova's excellent social network, Picasso met a number of highflying art dealers including Georges Wildenstein, Paul Rosenberg, J. Hessel and the brothers Gaston and Josse Bernheim. He thus entered the elite circle of people who did all their business over a bottle of champagne and flattered any new artist who had had recent success.

One who had achieved great success was Francis Scott Fitzgerald, a 24-year-old American, with his novel *This side of Paradise*. Fitzgerald had recently settled in France with his wife Zelda Sayre, also an author. The couple was introduced to Olga Koklova and Picasso and, during a season, the two couples went out together, accompanied by a third couple, the Beaumonts, who were known because they were titled nobility.

These new and favoured relations obliged Picasso to desist from further excursions to the wild regions that had attracted him since his youth. The holiday location that every high class Parisian dreamed of was the «Midi» and, more concretely, the *Côte d'Azur* («Blue Coast») that had then become fashionable. There, on the Mediterranean beaches, Picasso momentarily experienced the salty flavour of his childhood in Malaga once again and painted a series of fat bathers, that recall, although deformed and distant as they were, the fat nude matrons of Rubens. His wife had also swollen; she was some months pregnant, which must have excited the imagination of the painter. In February 1921 Paulo was born; he would be the only legitimate son of Picasso. Although the arrival of the baby increased the honourable status of the couple within the circles in which they moved, paternal happiness did not last long and a growing discomfort nibbled inside the artist.

Part four

The reservoir at Horta. Summer, 1909

Landscape at Ceret. Ceret, 1913

Sleeping paesants. Barcelona, 1919

Woman with hat, 1962

Lady in waiting (Margot). Paris, 1901

Motherhood.
Barcelona, 1903

Arlequin.
Barcelona, 1917

The pitgeons. Cannes, 1957

The Meninas, 1957

Self-portrait, 1906

The Mad. Barcelona, 1904

The blind guitarist. Barcelona, 1903

Portrait of Senyora Canals. París, 1905

Els quatre gats. Barcelona, 1899-1900

Portrait of Jaume Sabartés. Royan, 1939

The Meninas, 1957

Bather with beach ball, 1932

The Meninas, 1957

14

In the summer of 1922, Picasso, a satisfied father, did a drawing titled *Mère et fils* (« Mother and son», Cone Collection, The Baltimore Museum of Art) in which the similarity to the image of his son Paulo on the lap of his mother was evident.

In 1924, Picasso, a tormented husband, painted the oil on canvas *Paul en arlequin* («Paulo, dressed as a harlequin», Musée Picasso, Paris). The painting of his son disguised as a comic theatre character is realist and brightly coloured but only as far as the ankles. The feet of the child, as well as the legs of the seat which he is sitting on, are just suggested by a pencil sketch. The author thus left the work incomplete. He had once more managed to lose the serenity he had experienced, and the marriage faltered, just as Sra María Picasso López, the artist's mother, had predicted.

Seeking a new path, Picasso looked towards the Surrealists who, led by the writer André Breton, were beginning to make a mark in the French capital with activities never before witnessed. «What the Surrealist movement gave Picasso», writes the expert Marilyn Mc Cully, «was a series of new themes, overall erotic, which acted as a reinforcement of the disturbing elements already found in the work of Picasso». The multiple variations on the bathers theme, with there openly sexual and twisted forms, clearly show the impact of surrealism; in other works, the drawings and paintings of the *Crucifixió*, created between 1930 and 1935, the effect of distortion on the emotions of the spectator, can in some ways be interpreted as one of the psychological objectives of surrealism. In the 30's, Picasso, lik the Surrealist writers, played with the idea of metamorphism. For example, the image of the minotaur, the monster of Greek mythology, half man, half bull, that has traditionally been considered as the personification of the fight between the human and the animal, appears in Picasso's work, not only as an evocation of the idea, but also as a kind of self portrait.

An unexpected worry was added to the domestic conflicts of the artist in the form of Fernande Olivier, his first «fiancée», whose image appeared on the pages of *Le Soir*, one of the newspapers with the largest circulation in Paris. Picasso was livid.

Hélène Klein, curator of the Picasso Museum in Paris explains that, during a week in September 1930, *Le Soir* published a series of articles under the general title *Quand Picasso était pompier* (literally, «When Picasso was a fireman», but the word pompier, in French modernist circles, articulated a scornful disparagement of academy trained painters, considered as «retrogrades»).

The articles were signed by Fernande Olivier, a name

that at the time meant nothing to the average reader. A quarter of a century had passed since the «belle Fernande» had separated from the Malagan painter and the new generation was unaware of the intimacies and picaresque adventures of the small groups of bohemian artists at the beginning of the 20th century. However, the readers followed with interest the spontaneous prose of Fernande, which described the adventures of her youth with a now married father who belonged to the bourgeoisie of the Champs Elysées.

It seemed that Fernande did not explain all that she could have and the prestigious Parisian magazine *Le Mercure de France* became interested and offered Fernande the chance to complete her story with further chapters. The proposal was accepted and a second edition was published in the summer of 1931 under the titles *Neuf ans chez Picasso. Picasso et ses amis* (« Nine years with Picasso. Picasso and his friends»); *La naissance du cubisme* («The birth of Cubism») and *L'atelier du boulevard de Clichy* («The workshop on Clichy boulevard). The readers' interest was growing and the publishers encouraged Fernande to continue writing, which she did, publishing, in October 1933, the book *Picasso et ses amis*, («Picasso and his friends») more personal than the previous articles, in which the author, tender, nostalgic and sincere, confessed: «The most precious years of my life are the ones that I spent with Picasso... They are also, those where I lost a part of my youth and all my illusions».

Minotaur raping a Woman, 1933

Annoyed and indignant, Picasso took steps to avoid distribution of the book. But he was unable to stop it and Olga, his wife, jealous of her predecessors and fearing the loss of respectability, was even more displeased than he was. She probably suffered alone or shared confidences with intimate friends. Picasso, on the other hand, opted to spend more time out of the house than in it. Unknown to Olga, he had bought a 17th century castle in Boisgeloup in Normandy and its wide rooms served as workshop for the artist, and also as a love nest for extramarital relations. The new chosen one was Marie Thérèse Walter, a French girl in her twenties, blond, with a slender form and northern features, as can be seen in a photograph that Picasso took on a beach in 1929.

«Pablo Picasso met Marie Thérèse one day on the

street, near the Galleries Lafayette, when she was seventeen years old», Françoise Gilot explains in her memoirs. «The girl became the luminous representation of youth that fed Pablo's work. She was only interested in sports and did not intrude into his public or intellectual life. When Pablo did made social visits, he would go accompanied by Olga Koklova. When he was tired or exasperated, Marie Thérèse was always available to console him...and during a period of eight or nine years, the image of the girl appeared in many painting, drawings, sculptures and engravings. She was the privileged body on which the light fell perfectly. Marie Thérese, who was expecting a child, was the dream and Olga the reality, but in getting rid of Olga, reality changed. Marie Thérèse replaced Olga... In the picture *Guernika*, the woman with a fat head who emerges from the window

Marie Thérèse Walter

101

and holds a light with one hand, is clearly based on Marie Thérèse.»

That Picasso changed lovers would not surprise those who knew him intimately. It is surprising, however, that a woman as beautiful as Walter served as model for a work that depicts a beast like the Minotaur. It is difficult to find an explanation. The American Picasso expert, Arianna Stassinopoulos has advanced a possible psychological explanation: «The minotaur is nothing more than the subconscious of man.»

Pregnant with the child of Picasso, who had separated from Olga Koklova in 1935, Marie Thérèse Walter had a child, a girl, to whom she gave the exotic name Maya. At the same time, in Paris there was another woman, a photographer, who it seems, was waiting to meet someone as special as Picasso.

The photographer was sitting, motionless, on the terrace at one of the marble coffee tables, surrounded by waiters with black ties. She appeared distracted but was still aware of the approach of one such special man, no other than Picasso.

PART FIVE

15

Under the large green and white parasols on the terrace of the *Les Deux Magots* cafe, situated on a corner in the sixth district, the great and the good of the Parisian *Gauche Divine* met: so-called poets who wrote in prose, liberal dandies, avantguard artists, beautiful ladies, photographers with a taste for psychology, Freudian philosophers and out of work foreigners, cosmopolitans on holiday or those established in Paris.

It was a photographer of the group, called Dora

Dora Maar taked by Man Ray

Maar, who caught Picasso's attention that day. «The dice was thrown» says the historian Mary Ann Caws. «The painter felt an incredible attraction for this dark haired, tall, mysterious woman who was inclined to behave in strange ways» The writer Jean-Charles Gateau adds «Picasso felt a sudden violent attraction...Behind the haughty and enigmatic attitude of this woman, he saw a repressed spontaneity, a fiery temperament, a boldness and a delirium on the point of undoing her».

The dangerous mutual attraction between the photographer and the painter developed into an intermittent relationship. Some days they spent together in the artist's workshop, others, when things were not so good, separated each in their own house.

Picasso continued paying a subsidy both to Olga, his legitimate wife, as well as to Marie-Thérèse Walter, his last love, but from that point on his muse and lover would be Dora Maar, or Theodora Maar, born of a Croatian father and French mother now separated. She had lived for some time in Argentina and spoke Castilian, which is one of the things which without doubt contributed to the understanding between the couple.

The works completed by Picasso during the time he spent with Dora Maar are highly prized by the museums in which they are kept, in particular *Gernika* a huge black and white canvas, more than 7 and a half metres in length by 3 and a half metres in height, which references the destruction of the same Basque martyr city in April 1937 by German aviators from the Condor legion in the service of Franco. The work was created as a commission for the Spanish Republican Government, who also provided Picasso with a large studio in *Grands Augustins* Street, so that he could work more comfortably and rapidly, as the canvas was to be exhibited in the Spanish Pavilion at the «International Exhibition of Paris 1937», near to the USSR's pavilion presided over by the hammer and sickle, and that of Germany with its swastika.

The painting Guernika evidently refers to the disasters of the war, but the art critic André Fermigier also sees allusions to the minotour in the head of the bull depicted in the upper left hand part of the composition and at the same time references to the *corrida de toros* in the wounded horses head which neighs terrifyingly in the upper centre part of the composition.

Nine months previously the Spanish Civil War had begun between the Republican side with the support of the Soviets, and the *franquistas* who had the support of the Nazis. Given these alliances, Spain became the practice ground for the Second World War.

In the streets of Paris people were notably worried, and inside the workshop in *Grands Augustin*s Street, Picasso and Dora Maar lived a rather claustrophobic life. Dora had her own apartment but she visited the artist's workshop very frequently and collaborated with him, taking photographs, painting and modelling for him.

The oil on canvas *Femme en pleurs* («Woman crying», Penrose Collection, London) is inspired, it seems, in the distressed face of Dora Maar. It is a very dramatic painting which is hardly surprising given the circumstances and the taciturn and complex character of Picasso, to whom is attributed the phrase: «Painting is not done to decorate apartments. Painting is an instrument of war..».

The phantom of war is normally preceded by famine. And so it was. The shockwave of the world economic crisis of 1929 affected the economies of both defeated Germany and victorious France. The North American journalist, Hubert Renfro Knickerbocker, German correspondent for the New York Evening Post reported in the Winter of 1931-32 that the Berlin families of unemployed workers «were in a real state of famine...with the diet they live on it will not be long before they die».

The situation in France was certainly better, but in the summer of 1934, disturbing symptoms were detected, those isolated happenings, which announce the breakdown of the system. A paradigmatic example: in a local town gymnasium in Ronsard street in Montparnasse, a soup kitchen had been set up to allow the poor to eat good hot food at least once a day. The clients? There were none of the tramps who lived under the Sena bridge, nor factory workers, but intellectuals, generally well dressed, writers, unemployed musicians and a doctor who had lost everything; until recently he had a had his own thankful clientele, and now was incapable of paying for his own medical treatment.

The international situation worsened when in

1938, at the Munich conference, France and Great Britain gave in to the emerging power of Hitler, but after the invasion of Poland by Hitler, were reluctantly obliged to declare war on Germany.

Faced with the danger of the German invasion, certain well to do Parisian artists and intellectuals fled the French capital and took refuge in the Bordeaux region, which they believed to be safer. The Catalan painter Salvador Dali and his muse Deluvina Diakonoff, called Gala, fled to Arcachon, close to Bordeaux. Picasso rented a house in the coastal city of Royan, also close to Bordeaux and 300km from Paris, and stayed there for a short time waiting for news and making rapid return visits to the capital. He was extremely worried and doubts were overtaking him. If the Spanish state abandoned its neutrality and General Franco allied with Hitler , Picasso, as a Spanish citizen resident in Paris, would become a potential enemy for the French authorities, and as such liable to end up in a concentration camp with his belongings confiscated.

Due to the First World War, and in an identical situation, the German merchant Kahnweiler had avoided detention by fleeing to Switzerland, but his belongings which were in France, and considered enemy belongings, were confiscated and later auctioned.

What would Picasso do?

16

To save his skin and his belongings, an idea came to Picasso which he had always rejected: to solicit French nationality. He did it in a letter dated 3rd April 1940: «Dear Minister of Justice, I write with the honour of asking for French nationality...»

The painter gave his official address as 23 *La Boétie* Street, in the district of *La Madeleine* in Paris, the commissioner of which, impressed by the brilliant economic situation of the petitioner, owner of a castle, wrote a favourable report for the artist underlining the fact that «he has adopted our customs (the French ones) and has paid 700.000 francs in taxes in the year 1939».

The condition of *Monsieur* Picasso as a great contributor to French finance did nothing to dazzle the Chief Inspector of *Renseignements Généraux* («Secret Services»). In fact, it was quite the contrary.

The *Renseignements Généraux* had kept all documents relating to Picasso since he had first set foot in Paris in 1901 when he had stayed with his friend Pere Manyac, a Catalan anarchist, at the time in hiding in the French capital. The police report of the 18th June of the same year states that «Picasso shares the ideas of his compatriot Manach (or Manyac). As a consequence, he too should be considered an anarchist».

Given these far off beginnings and adding the police's observation of Picasso throughout the years, the Inspector of the *Renseignements* reported that, in a recent conversation over coffee, he had been heard apologising for the soviets and «as much as the painter is a modernist, he has created in France a situation which has allowed him to earn a great deal of money —saved, it appears in foreign banks and has become the owner of a castle in Gisors. Despite this, he has kept his extremist ideas, verging on communism. As a consequence he has no right to obtain French nationality...and on the contrary, he should be considered suspicious from a national point of view. « (All this documentation was exhibited in May 2004, in the Museum of the Chief of Police in *la Montagne-Sainte-Geneviève* Street and later toured around police headquarters in other French towns.)

The refusal of French nationality momentarily disorientated Picasso. Some artists such as Salvador Dalí, Max Ernst, André Masson, Ossip Zadkine and the intellectual André Breton, had fled to the United States, but others had decided to stay in Paris or other French cities like the couple made up of Jean-Paul Sartre and Simone de Beauvoir and, among others, the Barcelonian poster painter Carles Fontserè.

If Picasso didn't know what to do, fate would decide for him —he would stay in Paris.

On 14th June 1940, the Germans entered the French capital and beating their drums paraded in La Concorde square before raising the swastika on the bell tower of the Eiffel Tower.

As France had surrendered and was unarmed, there were no armed conflicts at the beginning of the occupation. Carles Fontserè explains in his memoirs the «The German soldiers entered Paris on the arm of the French soldiers and economic activity continued as usual. Electricity and the telephone lines functioned as normal... There was a great deal of intellectual and cultural life in occupied Paris...Jean-Paul Sartre began to be known in those years and Albert Camus left Algeria for the express reason of presenting, with success, his work.» He adds that «Hans Speidel, head of the German occupation in Paris met with French artists and intellectuals, among whom was the dandy Jean Cocteau.»

The memoirs of Fontserè, although believable, do not give an exactly true picture. A less idyllic vision is given by Pere Guilanyà, one of the many Catalan writers who had taken refuge in France, in a letter to a friend dated 16th January 1941: «If a miracle doesn't happen soon in Paris, it will be destroyed by the cold, hunger and all the other earthly miseries which are no less cruel.» In May, the man of letters Sebastian Gasch, another member of the group, found himself having to form a queue outside the door of a soup kitchen which offered a hot *Soupe Populaire*, a «popular dinner» once a day.

Meanwhile, Picasso, shut up in his workshop, did

not cease activity. As well as a bronze sculpture of the head of Dora Maar, in 1941 he painted a realist portrait of Nush, a young German friend of Paul Éluard, after his separation from Gala, the women who would be the eternal muse of Dali. Nush who performed acrobatics in a travelling circus, was a delicate woman, thin or almost skeletal. The painter depicted her with an inexpressive face, like a marble sculpture, with half closed eyes, a nude body and the breasts of a child painted in soft blue tones the same as those he had used in his youthful paintings of wandering acrobats.

The work of Picasso had been included by the Nazis in the category of «degenerated art» and the artist was prohibited from exhibiting in public. From time to time he was visited by a squad of uniformed soldiers, accompanied by a supposed art historian and a photographer. The squad presented itself with the same cold behaviour as had plenty of tax inspectors before them, and in their searches they turned the workshop upside down with a Teutonic precision, a difficult task in a space where disorder reigned.

Of a completely different nature was the visit, in 1942, of the aristocratic writer Ernst Jünger, famous for his first book, more journalism than fiction , *In Stahlgewittern* («Storms of steel»). Jünger maintained his distance from the Nazis, although he was obviously one of the German occupants. Following the Swiss historian Philippe Burrin, lecturer at the l'*Institut Universitaire des Hautes Études Internationaux* in Ginebra, who has made detailed studies of the French and German archives on Picasso, Picasso said to Jünger «If it depended solely on the two of us, sitting here in tranquillity, we would negotiate peace this very afternoon.»

Arno Breker, a German sculptor, although culturally frenchified also paid tribute to Picasso in a visit in 1942. Breker, 20 years younger than the Malagan, had lived for longer than 6 years in Paris. He had met Jean Cocteau and artists like Maurice Vlaminck and Constantin Brancusi. Highly influenced by the work of Rodin, and by classicism he had developed a strong friendship with Aristides Maillol, the unforgettable sculptor of *Banyuls-sur-Mer*, a Catalan coastal village under French administration. According to Volker Probst, Brekers biographer, the German sculptor helped Picasso get over his feeling of being threatened, a fact which is collaborated by James Lord, a writer of whom Picasso had drawn a perfect picture.

Under foreign occupation, the daily life of the French was not quite the same as it has been presented in many French and American films.

The real panorama was more complex, more varied and more doubtful.

In his theses P Burrin concludes that besides the «collaborators» or open supporters of Nazism, there were many others who flirted with the ideology, whether for conviction, weak moral fibre, necessity, lack of courage or other reasons.

However it seems that the vast majority of the population passively accepted the German occupation until the summer of 1943. André Gide wrote «To agree with the enemy is not cowardice but prudence». Jean-Paul Sartre, who had studied in Germany and been inspired by the German Heidegger, published his main work *L'être et le néant* without problems as well as publishing and directing plays whilst his partner Simone de Beauvoir said «I haven't seen hate in anyone. I've seen panic amongst the country folk, but when the fear has dissipated, they look at the Germans with eyes full of gratitude». The occupiers accepted the publication, by Louis Aragon, in 1942, of the novel *Les voyageurs de l'impériale* (The travellers of the Empire) and Jean Cocteau wrote «Each people has its own artistic and cultural conceptions. The occupying authorities hope to preserve the originality of the country and it is for this reason that French artists are allowed their freedom».

Picasso did manage to conserve his freedom, but his old friend Max Jacob was not so lucky. Recluse as he was in the monastery of Saint-Benoit-sur-Loire, under the protection of the abbot Monsenyor Weill, the Nazis followed his trail and he was confined in a Jewish concentration camp in Drancy where he died and was buried in a Jewish cemetery.

Max Jacob had been a special man. «In his sincere conversion to Christianity, Max understood that if you wanted to live like Christ, you had to abandon your liberal friends» reported a friend of his, Pierre Andreu. In 1921, he left Paris and went to live in Saint-Benoit-sur-Loire, which is situated some 150 km to the south of

Paris. There he had been able to vent in writing some of the internal torments which bothered him in letters to his friends. In one of these he wrote: «It is necessary to be Christian to know the devil. It is something horrible. My life is a life of suffering, I can no longer sin with pleasure and am full of remorse. It is true that the joys of union with God are infinite, but one must stop sinning and this will never happen at random. Here in the countryside there is no sin and the people pray.»

It is Pierre Salmon who has said that «Under Nazi occupation, Max Jacob ardently hoped for liberation, which would at the same time be the end of the martyrdom of his family and his race»

In September 1943, 2 months after allied troops had begun their invasion of Italy, Picasso was extremely busy sculpting and printing at the same time as the portraitist Brassaï was photographing his work, his friends and the ambience that surrounded him in the discrete shadow of his strange secretary and childhood friend, the Catalan Jaume Sabartés.

But Picasso, despite his 63 years could not help himself, when he did venture out into the streets, from turning his head to young women. There had been a considerable number of women in his life, one substituted for another. And now, as the occupation ended, two new young women, both French, were on the waiting list for entry into the circle of the painter.

One was called Françoise Gilot, and the other Geneviève Laporte.

17

The German army did not definitively surrender to the Allies until May 1945, but by August 1944 the troops of General de Gaulle together with the resistance organized by the communists, were victoriously entering Paris where the orgasmic happiness of *la Libération* was inevitably accompanied by *l'épuration* (the purge).

In the heat of the revived and exalted French patriotism, the heavy cultural tradition of the capital resurfaced, the *France éternelle* retook the wheel.

The Paris tradition of organising the annual so called *Salon d'Automne* («Autumn Salon») had persisted, a huge exhibition of painting, in which was exhibited the work of a single artist, almost always French, and chosen from many possibilities. In autumn of 1944, in honour of the circumstances, the exhibition, opened on the 6th October, was called *Salon de la Libération*, but, as a great surprise, the chosen artist was not French, but the Spanish author of *Gernika*, which somewhat disconcerted the French patriots. As if for emphasis, the Parisian papers headlined, on the 5th October (48 hours before the opening) that Picasso had joined the P.C.F. (French Communist Party).

In the exalted climate of this period, groups of discontented French provoked violent incidents in the Salon and the police had to protect the works of Picasso which were exhibited there. Some protested because the artist was not French. Others because the exhibited paintings did not follow the traditional line of great French painting which they knew from the Louvre. Fontanel, art critic for the magazine Gavroche, made comments which can be resumed as: «Shouldn't we have given importance to this first Salon de la Liberacion?» A salon which was supposed to be especially French, a free salon, which should have expressed the true thought and culture of France.»

Other protestors, people from the villages who had never in their lives seen either paintings or drawings by Picasso, naively saw the cubist works as a wasted joke in bad taste or, still worse, a jeer at good feeling.

The scandal made waves in the international press,

Gernika, 1937

118

including the North American *Time Magazine*, and Picasso, affected by the adverse atmosphere which surrounded Paris, and pulled by uncontrollable desires, decided that a change of air was needed and moved to the Provence coast with his new muse, Françoise Gilot.

And the other women he temporarily left behind?

The sweet Marie Thérèse Walter, who he visited often, may have missed him, but she had her subsistence assured. For Dora Maar, who was inside a psychiatric clinic, he bought a house.

And Olga, his legitimate wife, would simply have more difficulty in sending him the pathetic wounded letters which she addressed to him, like the one which said: «What a great painter you would be, Pablo, if you painted like Rembrandt!»

The Picasso-Gilot couple first moved to the castle Grimaldi, a 16th century fortress which presided over a view of the Antibes and a large part of the Costa Brava, and then to a house in Vallauris, to the west of the head of the Antibes.

The time in Provence reveals itself as very fruitful and innovative in the work of Picasso. The title of the painting *Joie de vivre* («The joy of life»), painted in 1946, clearly expresses the momentary state of mind of the artist, while a red ceramic piece from 1947, representing the bull, reminds us of the old, permanent delirium for the *corridas de toros* of his Malagan infancy, mixed with an obsession for the mythological bull become the terrifying minotaur.

With four simple brushstrokes, the artist decorated a series of elaborated ceramic plates in Vallauris, which represented schematically a serene or smiling face. In other words, he was content. And if, in his works, pictures of fauns and centaurs accompanied a nymph, it means to say that the woman of his current dreams was young.

Françoise Gilot was 23 when she met Picasso. She was a slender woman, with marked features, thick hair, lively eyes, a pointed nose and certain male features. Her forehead suggested great intelligence, and in her own explanations, which she gave with details in the 60s in her book *Life with Picasso* she is seen to have an extremely rational mentality like many fashionable French intellectuals of the time. Only child of a rich businessman, she was keen on drawing and painting and from there came her interest in Picasso.

But the prolific and promiscuous patriarch could not entirely escape his growing family. In 1947 Claud, the first son of Françoise Gilot was born. In 1949 she gave birth to a second child who was named Paloma.
The same year Paul (or Paulo) Picasso, the son of Olga Koklova and the artist, married to the ceramicist Émilienne Lotte also had a child, baptised with the name Pablo although he was always called «Pablito». The following year the couple had a second child, a girl baptised with the name Marina.

There were a lot of mouths to feed. However, the fortune of Picasso was valued at 200 million French Francs.

Françoise Gilot with Picasso taked by Robert Capa

«In that period, Picasso's growing fame attracted many visitors (to his house in the Costa Brava)» —says Marylyn McCully— «and some, overall Louis Aragon, encouraged him to get more involved in politics». The simple drawing he did of a white pigeon in flight was used as a logo on the poster which advertised the World Peace Congress which took place in Wroclaw, Poland in 1949, therefore within the Soviet orbit, and in London in 1950 and later reproduced in numerous posters and publications.

In 1951 the Soviet Union awarded Picasso the Stalin Peace Prize, which not only increased his fame across the continents, but also, as James Lord has remarked «increased the price of his paintings».

PART SIX

18

The Second World War was over and the baths at Antibol, the ancient Antipolis of 340 AC, had recovered their prestige. Distinguished clients visited to remedy their illnesses, whether imaginary or real and Picasso thought that this could be the pleasant place he was looking for.

There are a handful of his paintings, drawings and ceramic pieces now in the museum at Antibol, which has the name *Musée Picasso*. Among the pieces kept there, apart from the painting *La Joie de Vivre,* are an oval ceramic plate entitled *Plat au Minotaure et au Centaure Combattant* («Minotaur and Centaur in combat»); the oil painting *Ulysse et les Sirènes* and the pencil *Faune dansant dans l'eau* («Faun dancing in water») and *Faune debout jouant de la diaule* («Faun playing an instrument»).

The titles of these pieces, like others created at Vallauris, are more playful than his main themes, such as the Minotaur, commonly associated with the bull, a beast firmly rooted in Iberian prehistory. The same beast that the *banderillero* and the *picador* torture in the «Plaza de toros» in a distant echo of the Roman Circuses, before the *matador*, or *torero*, gives it the final mortal wound...provided the wounded animal doesn't kill the man first with its horns.

It is due to the latent influence of the *espagnolades* (Spanishified) wrote Prosper Mérimée in the 19th Century, that bullfights had and have a certain acceptance in the South East corner of France. Picasso also contributed with his affection for the bull. When he was only 8 years old he painted in oil on wood a tiny canvas titled *El picador*, and at 9 years of age completed a drawing titled *La corrida* («The Bullfight», Museu Picasso de Barcelona), which is innocent bit very realistic and was drawn form real life on a visit to a bullfight in Malaga.

Françoise Gilot allowed him to follow this vein. One day in October 1946 Picasso painted a pastel, wax and coloured pencil portrait of her, schematic but realistic and pleasant to the eye. The model is depicted extremely serenely; the only detail which stands out is the symbol, marked in red pencil on the highest point of the woman's forehead —of the crossed hammer and sickle. The portrait is actually titled *Portrait de Françoise avec la Faucille et le Marteau* («Portrait of Françoise with hammer and sickle»).

Not far from Antibol, in the locality of Vence, the decoration on the chapel of the Rosari of the old Dominican convent in the area was inaugurated with painted murals by Henri Matisse, the painter famous for his strong audacious colours, known by and rival to Picasso.

Other famous artists had painted in these old religious buildings: Roualt, Chagall, Léger, Bonnard had done so in the Assis church (Umbria, Italy) and Braque at Varengeville (Normandy). Picasso had never been asked to do this type of work, but, not to be outdone by his famous rivals, and helped by his social standing, he managed to convince them to let him paint murals in the Roman chapel of Vallauris, which had been desecrated since the antireligious furore of the French Revolution.

Using the opposite concepts of war and peace, which Picasso had obviously drawn from the title of the most famous of Tolstoy's works, he worked feverishly on the new project, which consisted in depicting on the left hand wall of the entrance to the nave, the disasters of war, and on the right the joy of peace. He used a method which entailed painting pieces of the mural on to flexible fabric which was then attached to the nave walls.

The final result is a piece which is difficult to interpret and unlike anything painted by his competitors. According to the erudite North American Picassian Gertje R. Utley, in the dark colours of the left hand wall where there is a predominance of black, one can see «the charioteer, the personification of war, a naked being, a hybrid with a male body and a head which has often been described as half owl, half minotaur...Behind the charioteer there is a shadowy army holding daggers, swords and hatchets...and on the right, a vision of paradise».

Working on this piece during long periods isolated in his workshop, Picasso left Françoise Gilot and their two children to one side, and relations between the two deteriorated. It appeared to Françóise Gilot that the artist was having «adventures» with his old friend Geneviève Laporte and, as well as that, she now understood that the prophetic advice which Dona Maria Picasso had, many years ago given to Olga Koklova, would come true in an infallible way: «Pablo will never make a woman happy».

Françoise Gilot had not been educated to bring up children. Neither her grandparents nor her mother had taught her anything about it. She demonstrated a strict Cartesian logic like that of any Sorbonne trained intellectual, but as relationships are not based on logical reason but on sentiments, emotions, obsessions, instincts and subconscious impulses, her life with Picasso was full of twists, misunderstandings and disgust, which are reflected in her memoirs. These memoirs describe intimate details of the character of Picasso and those who surrounded him. The description of Jaume Sabartés, for example, the silent and perpetual secretary of the Malagan, is the best that has been written about him and presented like a character in a gothic novel.

In 1953, Gilot abandoned Picasso and returned to Paris with her two children. However the hole created in the life of Picasso was quickly filled by Jacqueline Roque, a woman of 27 years of age, who worked as an assistant in a ceramic studio and had a child from a previous relationship. It is true that the woman was not entirely aware of what she was letting herself in for, but with her docile character one could have said that she would have more patience with the artist than her predecessors, as young girls who marry older men often do.

Something would happen, however, to disturb the Arcadian peace at Vallauris. The unfortunate Olga Koklova, with whom Picasso had not been in contact for almost two decades, had been taken into hospital in Cannes with cancer. Olga, a devotee of the Orthodox Church, died aged 64 in 1955. Her situation was demonstrated by the fact that instead of being buried in Cannes where there was an orthodox cemetery, she was buried in Vallauris «a place which she hated» as Françoise Gilot states in her memoirs, «because she associated it with my relationship with Picasso».

Isolated from the headaches of domestic life, which were however, piling up, the Malagan had plunged into adding the final touches to the murals which were installed in the chapel at Vallauris in 1954. The artist hoped for praise as had happened four years ago when the local authorities had discovered the sculpture *L'home del xai* installed in the Main Square in Vallauris. It would not be the same. For unexplainable reasons, the doors of the chapel were locked and remained so for five years.

In a state of bad humour, one day in 1956, Picasso was surprised by an unexpected visit which moved his conscience. Marcelle Braque, the wife of Georges Braque, painting companion of his youth, came to see him, as an intermediary, on the part of his first love Fernande Olivier. the woman from the *Bateau-Lavoir* in Montmartre. The «beautiful Fernande», now 74 years old, lived in misery and was half blind. Years earlier she had asked Picasso for help but he hadn't replied. Now, if the Malagan didn't help her, she threatened to publish unedited letters and documents, which she had, for discretionary reasons, left out of her book *Picasso et ses amis,* documents which would compromise his reputation. Frightened, Picasso said to the intermediary, Marcelle Braque, that if she refrained from publishing the documents he would provide her with a modest pension until she died. According to Marcelle Braque, Fernande accepted the offer.

. The reputation of the artist was indemnified and the following year he received a commission to paint murals in an enormous building of worldwide fame, the headquarters of UNESCO in Paris, but, in part due to his bad conscience over the issue of Fernande, he continued to feel frustrated with the chapel at Vallauris which would not open, they had told him, until July 1958.

Part seven

19

Paris, July 14, 1958. The tricolour republican flag flies in the avenues, boulevards, squares and balconies of the capital. It is the French National Festival. It was also around this date that the public opening and inauguration of the chapel at Vallauris decorated by Picasso was announced and promoted by the Communist Movement for Peace.

The days passed and confirmation of the inauguration did not arrive.

The Mayor of Vallauris nervously awaited news from Paris.

The news which finally arrived was not what had been expected. The 4th Republic had entered a crisis. General Charles De Gaulle was being called to form a new government and had named as Minister of Cultural and Intellectual affairs, the political activist in the resistance against Nazism and art writer André Malraux, which meant he was unable to carry out the inauguration at Vallauris under the auspices of the communists.

The act finally took place on the 19th September

1959, presided over, in the absence of Malraux and to the disappointment of Picasso, by a delegate from the Ministry. In a great show of diplomacy, intended to reduce the slight felt by the Spanish artists, the delegate gave a long speech in which he eulogised about the work, saying that «In the future, people will come to see the Chapel at Vallauris in the same way that they visit Lascaux», referring to the caves close to Montignac in Dordogne which contain prehistoric paintings of bulls, bison and other animals as well as humans and which was becoming a world tourist attraction.

Picasso, however, was not satisfied by the speeches, and he let off steam by channelling his resentment into an oil painting more than a metre in height; *Nature morte à la Tête de Taureau* («Still Life of the Head of a Bull», Musée Picasso, Paris). The head of the beast, of a threatening nature, was supposed to symbolise, according to the erudite Gertje R. Utley, the figure of General De Gaulle after his return to power, but this time censored by those who had once applauded him.

Picasso was probably comforted when in 1962 the Soviet Union awarded him the Lenin Prize, at the same time as MOMA (Museum of Modern Art) in New York, exhibited a considerable number of his works despite the fact that the cold war was in full flow.

Picasso had always disliked explicit political declarations although his preferences were evident. In any case, it was in his painting that he expressed his inner self mixed with his reactions to external events. At the time

Picasso looking at a poster of Stalin at Rome el 1949

there was fear of armed confrontation between the United States and the Soviet Union and the possibility of nuclear war and it appears that it was this which the artist wanted to communicate with the killing shown in his painting *L'Enlèvement des Sabines* («The kidnapping of the Sabines», Musée National d'Art Moderne, Centre G. Pompidou, Paris).

Picasso, nearing 80 years of age, continued to demonstrate overflowing energy. Now that Olga Koklova had died, he could remarry. He had separated decades ago from his wife but had never asked her for a divorce because it would have meant sharing his fortune with her. He was, therefore a widow who wished to try his luck once more in marriage, this time with Jacqueline Roque. Given that there was a 45 year age difference, in order to avoid the press they were married in a secret civil ceremony one day in March 1961, by the state authorities in Vallauris, without guests.

As the changes in partner were always accompanied by changes in residence, the artist had to find a new home. At first he bought another castle, this time in Vauvenargues, a village in Aix-en-Provence («Ais de Provença» in Occitan). But, a few months later, unsatisfied and feeling very isolated, he bought a fortified house called Notre-Dame-de-Vie («Mother of God of Life») in Mougins, near to Cannes and 85 km as the crow flies from Vauvenargues.

During his extended life Pablo Ruiz Picasso had lived in a huge number of places, but he had never put down roots. The happy Arcadia of Provence had proved to be a summer dream. Despite this, it was in these Provence corners blown by the north-west wind and where he had made many friends, where he had sown his seed and where an inner voice told him he should stay.

It was in Cannes that Olga had died and his grandchild Marina had been born. In Antibol, near to Cannes, Françoise Gilot left her mark. In the main square of Vallauris, the statue *L'Homme au mouton* («Man with sheep») had been installed on a plinth to the applause of his party comrades, probably without understanding its real meaning. Picasso and his friends called themselves atheists, but the image of the man with sheep around his neck is taken from the evangelical parable of the «Good Shepherd», a fact which Picasso, more astute than his friends, was well aware of.

The change in family life, in the complex spirit of Picasso, also meant a change of objectives and artistic methods. Tired of ceramics, he tried a new technique: lino cuts, one of the most impressive of which is the colour print *Buste de femme avec chapeau* («Bust of a woman with hat», Museu Picasso de Barcelona).

167 portraits of Jacqueline Roque were painted by the artist in these years, who was a model as well as housekeeper. It is thought to be her who posed for the oil paintings *Las Meninas* («Court Ladies», Museu Picasso of Barcelona) and *Le déjeuner sur l'herbe* («Breakfast on the grass», Staatsgalerie, Stuttgart).

The two people who the artist could rely on in these years were Jacqueline Roque and his eternal personal secretary, the Barcelonian Jaume Sabartés. Sabartés, who was the same age as Picasso, donated, in agreement with the artist, 600 of his works —under the name Sabartés Collection— to Barcelona Council. They are kept in the Palau Aguilar (headquarters of the future Museu Picasso in Barcelona) and the donation was made in order to avoid the dispersal of the artist's works after the two had died.

In 1963, the artist was satisfied by the publication of a biography, authorised by himself, and written by Antonina Vallentin, and based to a large extent on the previously reported anecdotes of the book by Jaume Sabartés *Picasso, portraits et souvenirs*.

But one year later, the ground of the house where Picasso lived shook with the latest news: the prestigious

Rafael Alberti, Picasso, Luis Miguel Dominguín and Antonio
Gades in Cannes at 1966. Taked by Antonio Cores

North American publisher McGraw-Hill had just published *Life with Picasso,* a book written by Françoise
Gilot in which, in close to 350 pages, she describes intimate details of her life with the painter. English editions
of the book had already arrived in France. The attempts
of the artist to stop distribution were in vain. The scare
grew even bigger when the artist discovered that the
same publisher had also just finished editing an English
version of the 1933 book *Picasso et_ses amis* by the poor
Fernande Olivier, a work which the artist had been sim-
ilarly unable to stop. However, the English edition went
largely unnoticed amongst the French public.

On the contrary, the memoirs of Gilot were edited in
Paris, in French, in 1965 and became a best seller, con-
tributing to the revival of Picasso's fame and multiplying
the number of exhibitions of his work around the world:

In 1966 an exhibition of 1000 works in Paris, in 1968 another in the Sala Gaspar in Barcelona and in 1970 a third in the Palau dels Papes in Avingnon, Provence.

«Between 1967 and the first months of 1973, the invention and production of Picasso, which had always been abundant, became excessive» says J. Palau i Fabre, the devotee and constant student of the Malagan's work. «The drawing, printing, ceramics, painting and even the sculpture were worked on almost simultaneously...the freedom is total, both technically and conceptually. Eroticism, which had been one of his sources of inspiration, returned with a strange violence. La Celestina, a character from Castilian theatre who he had depicted during his youth in Barcelona, seems to have been following his steps and growing old at his side, like the old harlequins of his youth who had become old and toothless. Beside the rogue and a handful of ambiguous and truculent others, amongst them bullfighters, hat wearing Catalans, and old sleazes are metaphysical images...as well as some self portraits, in some cases intended, and in others involuntary, in the most moving of which Picasso, looking inside himself, tries to capture in his face his own death.»

20

Over fifty of Picasso's works were exhibited in the Sala Gaspar in Barcelona in March 1968 and the art critic Joan Cortés, in an article published in the newspaper «La Vanguardia» was not sparing in his praise: «It is the most substantial exhibition of the artist's work ever exhibited in our city... A superb example of an inexhaustible, courageous and aggressive creativity» wrote Cortès. «Picasso shows in his attitude a positive and fertile repulsion towards a direct vision of the world. He carried this antagonism in his blood and with his works, has influenced the history of modern art in unforeseen and unimagined ways...Jaume Sabartés, the great friend and secretary of the painter, has helped in the preparation of the exhibition, a collection of prints, lithographs and drawings, which is being shown at the Museu Picasso in Barcelona, the most important in the world of its genre.»

In May 1970, the news that the *Bateau-Lavoir*, the inhospitable house of wood in the Montmartre neighbourhood where Picasso had lived as a youth, had been demolished. J. Palau i Fabre, who at this time had been visiting Picasso on a regular basis to question him, asked what effect the news had had. Picasso replied: *Tant mieux!* («What a relief»).

Palau explains: «The answer disconcerted me. What did Picasso mean by his reply? Weren't all the memories of his youth contained in that place, of his years of bloody fighting in Paris? Wasn't it he who had said, years after leaving the *Bateau-Lavoir*, that he had never been as happy as he was there?».

The news was insignificant for the majority of the French public, and certainly for the generation of youths of May 1968 who were uninterested in the adventures of those who could have been their grandparents. For Picasso, on the other hand, who was an extremely superstitious man, the destruction of the place became mythical. It was a bad omen, and appeared to him a metaphor for his life as he neared ninety years of age. It may be that he was afraid of dying under the weight of his own passions like a medieval knight under the weight if his armour.

The *Bateau-Lavoir*! It must have woken up his imagination with huge number of memories, of good and bad times, of dreams evaporated in the mists of time which are only remembered in the uninterrupted stream of memoirs!

It was one day in spring when *la belle Fernande Olivier*, beauty of beauties, made a triumphant entrance into the life of the amazing bohemian painter who shone in the darkness. It was also a day in spring when the good natured Fernande left carrying nothing but a purse containing eleven French Francs.

It was December when he took the sweet and fragile Eva Gouel to Barcelona and presented her to his parents as his future wife. Eva, who had darned socks and knitted balaclavas for the soldiers and who later, died of cancer, all in the quietest possible way so as not to disturb the painter.

And after this came the supposedly «happy 20s» of free flowing champagne in which he married the ballerina Olga Koklova, went strolling in the company of Scott Fitzgerald and his wife along the Champs Élysées, in that imaginary corner of paradise, before meeting the curvaceous Marie Thérèse Walter, who was in turn substituted for the mysterious Dora Maar, the woman who cries for the martyred city of Guernika.

After the Spanish and World wars, the Parisian intellectual Françoise Gilot entered the Minotaurian labyrinth and lost herself until she managed to escape with her two children.

Towards the end of this labyrinthine journey, Jacqueline Roque silently enters the scene, the gentle wife, secretary, model and head of the castle, the last of the *Madame Picassos*, the seventh maiden of Picassian mythology.

Picasso died on the 8th April 1973 in Notre-Dame-de-Vie de Mougins and was buried two days later in Vauvenargues. We are not aware of any Malagan who called for him to be buried in his native city. In any case, he would never have returned.

It is impossible to know the workings of his mind

Jacqueline Roque at 1960

and the reasons for his behaviour. We can say, and here I cite Lord Byron, that «the mind can make Heaven from Hell or Hell from Heaven».

It is possible that the German dealer Kahnweiler was not the only man in the world who understood Picasso. It may be that the Catalan painter Joan Miró, a great friend of the Malagan also did, as we see in his declaration that «Picasso represented the final blow to a civilisation and a culture which were already out of date.»

In any case, Picasso has certainly been the only artist who has known how to live seven lives, and his path is unrepeatable.

CHRONOLOGY

1881
　Pablo Ruiz Picasso is born in Malaga (Andalusia).
1885
　Lola, the painter's sister, is born.
1887
　Concepción, the painter's second sister, is born.
1891
　Picasso's family moves to A Coruña (Galícia)
1895
Concepción dies at 7 years of age.
　Picasso paints the oil painting *Viejo pescador* in Malaga, a great work of realist painting. The Ruiz Picasso family move to Barcelona, where the father finds work as a drawing teacher at the School of Fine Arts.
1897
　Picasso's work *Ciencia y Caridad* wins a prize in the Exposició de Belles Arts in Madrid.
1900
　Accompanied by the painter Carles Casagemas, Picasso goes to Paris for the first time for the Universal Exhibition.

1901

The painter C. Casagemas commits suicide in Paris.

Works by Picasso are exhibited in the gallery of the French dealer A. Vollard.

1904

Picasso decides to live in Paris. The model Fernande Olivier becomes his lover.

1905

The Steins, North-American millionaires established in Paris, buy works by Picasso.

1906

Picasso spends time in Gósol (Spanish Catalonia) with Fernande Olivier.

1907

Picasso paints the cubist *Les Demoiselles d'Avignon*, in Paris, which will not be exhibited until 1916.

1909

The Parisian newspaper *Le Figaro* publishes *Le Futurisme*, the manifesto of the Italian intellectual F. T. Marinetti.

Workers revolt in Barcelona. 80 religious buildings are burnt by anarchists.

1911

Apollinaire, a friend of Picasso's, is imprisoned for the theft of various works from the Louvre.

1912

Picasso signs a contract with the German dealer M. Kanhweiler. The Russian collector Sergei Txukin (in English, Shchukin) buys some of his works.

Fernande Olivier and Picasso break off relations. The painter, with a new lover, Eva Gouel, spends time in Ceret (French Catalonia).

1913

José Ruiz Blasco, the father of the painter, is buried in Barcelona. Picasso and Eva return to Ceret.

1914

The First World War begins. The dealer Kahnweiler flees to Switzerland.

1915

Eva Gouel dies in Paris.

1916

The painting *Les Demoiselles d'Avignon* is exhibited for the first time in a Paris gallery.

1917

The Russian S. Diaghilev presents the ballet *Parade* in Rome with scenery painted by Picasso.

The October Revolution in Russia. The collector Txukin emigrates to Paris and the Bolsheviks seize the works he had by Picasso.

1918

End of the First World War.

Picasso marries the ballerina Olga Koklova in Paris.

1919

Picasso begins to make contact with high standing dealers. He donates the painting *L'Arlequí* to the city of Barcelona, where other works of his are being exhibited.

1921

Paul, son of the artist and Olga Koklova, is born.

The French government seizes the works of Picasso which are property of the German dealer Kahnweiler, as «enemy goods».

1924

Marinetti publishes *Futurismo e fascismo* in Rome.

1925

First exhibition of the surrealist collective in Paris.

1927

Marie-Thérèse Walter, becomes Picasso's new lover.

1930

In Paris Fernande Olivier publishes a series of articles about her life with Picasso.

1931

Picasso leaves Olga Koklova.

1932

The dealers Gaston and Josse Bernheim organise the first big retrospective of Picasso in the «Galerie Petit» in Paris.

1933

Fernande Olivier's memoirs, *Picasso et ses amis*, is published and infuriates the artist.

1934

The Museu d'Art in Catalonia opens a room dedicated to Picasso.

1935

Picasso completes the etching *Minotauromàquia*.

Maia Widmaier, daughter of Picasso and Marie-Thérèse Walter is born.

The Catalan Jaume Sabartés moves to Paris to become life-long secretary for Picasso.

1936

Dora Maar becomes Picasso's new lover.

The Spanish Civil War begins.

1937

Picasso paints the huge canvas *Gernika*, after the bombing of the village in the Basque Country by the Condor legion of the German air force in the service of Franco.

1938

Barcelona is bombed by the Condor legion.

1939

April: end of the Spanish Civil War. During the war or shortly afterwards, Picasso's mother dies in Barcelona.

September: the Second World War begins.

1940

Spring: Picasso applies for French nationality and is refused.

14th June: Hitler's troops invade Paris.

1943

Dora Maar breaks off relations with Picasso.

1944

25th August: General De Gaulle's troops liberate Paris.

Groups of Parisians protest at the «Salon d'Automne» in Paris where Picasso's work is exhibited, considering it a scandal of bad taste.

Picasso joins the PCF (French Communist Party).

1945

Dora Maar is taken into a psychiatric hospital.

1946

Françoise Gilot becomes Picasso's new lover.

1947

Picasso dedicates himself to ceramics.

Claude, son of Picasso and F. Gilot is born.

The «Cold War» begins.

1949

Pablito Picasso, son of Paul Picasso and Émilienne Lotte is born.

Paloma, daughter of the artist and F. Gilot is born.

The painter's fortune is valued at around 200 million French Francs.

1950

Marina Picasso, granddaughter of the painter and Olga Koklova is born in Cannes (Provence).

1951

The Soviet Union awards Picasso the *Stalin Peace Prize*. Geneviève Laporte becomes the artist's new lover.

1953

Françoise Gilot together with their two children leaves Picasso.

1954

Jacqueline Roque becomes the new friend of Picasso. The artist starts a series of paintings based on the works of Classic artists.

1955

Olga Koklova dies of ill health at 64 years of age in Cannes hospital and is buried in Vallauris.

1957

Picasso paints murals in the headquarters of UNESCO in Paris and donates 16 ceramic works to the city of Barcelona.

1959

The chapel at Vallauris (Provence), painted by Picasso, is opened.

1960

Jaume Sabartés, Picasso's secretary, proposes the opening of a Picasso Museum in Barcelona.

1961

Picasso marries Jacqueline Roque.

1962

The Soviet Union awards Picasso the *Lenin Prize*. Exhibition of the painter's work at the Museum of Modern Art, New York.

1963

The opening of the Palau Aguilar (Museu Picasso) in Barcelona with a series of works donated by the painter's secretary, J. Sabartés. The Spanish government refuses to allow the museum to be named after Picasso.

1964

Fernande Olivier's book, *Picasso et ses amis* is published in English.

Françoise Gilot publishes her book *Life with Picasso* in the United States.

1966

Picasso's works are exhibited in Paris.

Fernande Olivier dies of ill health at 84 years of age.

1968

Exhibition of prints, drawings and paintings in the Sala Gaspar in Barcelona.

1969

Exhibition of Picasso's works in the Palau dels Papes in Avignon (Provence).

1970

Picasso donates 1700 works from his youth to the city of Barcelona.

The «Bateau-Lavoir» is sunk in Montmartre.

1971

Exhibition of Picasso's works at the Louvre in Paris.

1973

Picasso dies on 8th April, aged 92 and is buried in the castle at Vauvenargues (Provence). His inheritance is shared between his dependents and the French State.

* * *

1973

Pablito Picasso commits suicide aged 24.

1975

Marie-Thérèse Walter commits suicide.

Paul Picasso, the artists's firstborn, dies of ill health.

1981

The Soviet government publishes a series of stamps depicting the image of Picasso.

1982

Jacqueline Roque, Picasso's widow, donates 41 ceramic pieces to Barcelona.

1986

Jacqueline Roque commits suicide.

1988

Souvenirs intimes, Fernande Olivier's book, is edited for the first time in Paris.

The birthplace of Pablo Ruiz Picasso in Malaga, is enlarged and becomes the headquarters of the Museo Picasso Foundation.

1989

The canvas *Au Lapin agile*, painted in 1905, depicting a scene of acrobats, is bought in New York for $40 million.

1990

Françoise Gilot moves to Austin, Texas (USA).

1998

Dora Maar dies of ill health.

1999

New rooms in the Museu Picasso in Barcelona are opened to the public.

2002

Marina Picasso's book *Picasso, Mon Grand-père* is published in Catalan

2003

The Museo Picasso in Malaga is opened with works donated or left by Christine, widow of Paul Picasso, first born of the painter.

The Museu Picasso in Barcelona is enlarged to 11.500 m2.

2004

«Picasso-Ingres» exhibition at the *Musée Picasso* in Paris.

«Dossiers Picasso» exhibition at the *Musée de la Préfecture de Paris*.

A canvas by Picasso is bought for almost $100million at an auction in Sotheby's, New York.

The Palau i Fabre Foundation in Caldes d'Estrac (Maresme, Catalonia) opens a centre of Picassian documents.

2006

125th anniversary of the artist's birth.

BIBLIOGRAFY

BERGER, John: *La réussite et l'échec de Picasso*. Denoël (Paris, 1968).

BOONE, Danièle: *Picasso*. Éditions Hazan (Paris, 1988).

BURRIN, Phillipe: *Francia bajo la ocupación nazi*. Ed. Paidós (Barcelona, 2004).

CALLICÓ, Ferran: *L'art i la revolució social*. (Barcelona, 1936).

CANYAMERES, Ferran: *Epistolari (1939-1951). Obra completa VI*. Columna (Barcelona, 1996).

CANYAMERES, Raymond: *Spain 1808-1939*. Oxford University Press (Oxford, 1966).

CANYAMERES, Joan: *Barcelona. La història*. Edicions de 1984. (Barcelona, 2001).

CAWS, Mary Ann: *Dora Maar with & without Picasso. A biography*. Thames and Hudson Ltd. (London, 2000).

CAWS, Alexandre: *Picasso. La seva vida i la seva obra / Su vida y su obra*. N. Editorial, S.A. (Barcelona, 1981).

CORTÈS I VIDAL, Joan: *Setanta anys de vida artística barcelonina*. Ed. Selecta (Barcelona, 1980).

COSTA CLAVELL, Xavier: *Picasso. Musée Picasso de Barcelona*. Ed.Escudo de Oro (Barcelona, s/d).

DAIX, Pierre: *La vie de peintre de Pablo Picasso*. Seuil (Paris, 1977).

— *Picasso, Dossiers de la Préfectures de Paris.* Acatos (Paris, 2003).

FONTSERÈ, Carles: *Un exiliat de tercera. A Paris durant la Segona Guerra Mundial.* Proa (Barcelona, 1999).

— *Paris, Mèxic, Nova York. Memòries 1945-1951.* Proa (Barcelona, 2005).

GATEAU, Jean-Charles: *Paul Eluard ou le frère voyant.* R. Laffont (Paris, 1988).

GILOT, Françoise and CARLTON LAKE: *Life with Picasso.* McGraw-Hill, Inc. (USA,1964).

HUGHES, Arnold: *The Social History of Art.* Routledge & Keagan Paul (London, 1951).

HUGHES, Robert: *El impacto de lo nuevo. El arte en el siglo XX.* Galaxia Gutenberg. Círculo de Lectores (Barcelona, s/d).

IZQUIERDO, Paula: *Picasso y las mujeres.* Belacqua (Barcelona, 2003).

JACKSON, Julian: *France. The dark years, 1940-1944.* Oxford University Press (London, 2001).

JACKSON, Paul: *Art. A new history.* Weidenfield and Nicolson (London, 2003).

MAIAR, Josep i VILALTA, Jaume: *Iconografia de la sardana en l'obra de Picasso.* Departament de Cultura. Generalitat de Catalunya (Barcelona, 1981).

MELIÀ, Josep: *Joan Miró.* Dopesa (Barcelona, 1971).

NONELL, Carolina: *Nonell.* Ed. Gustavo Gili (Barcelona, 1964).

O'BRIAN, Patrick: *Picasso. A Biography.* W.W. Norton (New York, London, 1994).

OLIVIER, Fernande: *Picasso et ses amis.* Éditions Stock (Paris, 1933).

— *Picasso et ses amis*, edited by Hélène Klein. Pygmalion (Paris, 2001).

— *Loving Picasso. The private journal of Fernande Olivier.* Abrams (New York, 2001).

PALAU I FABRE, Josep: *Picasso.* Edicions Polígrafa, S.A. i «la Caixa» (Barcelona, 1981).

— *Picasso a Catalunya.* Edicions Polígrafa (Barcelona, 1975).

— *Picasso, Barcelona, Catalunya.* Quaderns L'Avenç (Barcelona, 1981).

— *Querido Picasso.* Ed. Destino (Barcelona, 1997).

PICASO, Marina: *Grand-père.* Éditions Denoël (Paris, 2001). Traducció al català: *L'avi.* Pòrtic (Barcelona, 2002).

PLANES, Ramon: *El modernisme a Sitges.* Ed. Selecta (Barcelona, 1969).

POOL, Phoebe and BLUNT, Anthony.: *Picasso. The formative years. A study of his sources* (London, 1962).

PROBST, Volker G.: *Arno Breker. Biographie.* Jacques Damase, éditeur. (Cachan, France, Février 1981).

RICHARDSON, John: *A Life of Picasso, Vol. I: 1881-1906.* Random House (New York, 1991).

— *A Life of Picasso, Vol. 2: 1907-1917.* Random House (New York, 1996).

— *The Sorcerer's Apprentice: Picasso, Provence and Douglas Cooper.* Random House (New York, 1999).

SABARTÉS, Jaume: *Picasso en su obra* (Madrid, 1935).

— *Picasso. Portraits et souvenirs.* Vox Éditeurs (Paris, 1946).

SICKERT, Walter: *The Complete Writings on Art.* Oxford University Press (Oxford, 2001).

SOCIAS PALAU, Jaume: *Pintura catalana en el Castell de la Geltrú.* Ed. Selecta (Barcelona, 1977).

STASSINOPOULOS HUFFINGTON, Arianne: *Picasso. Creator and destroyer.* Simon and Schuster (New York, 1988).

STEIN, Gertrude: *Picasso.* La Esfera de los libros, S.L. (Madrid, 2002).

UTLEY, Gertje R.: *Picasso. The Communists years.* Yale University Press (Yale, USA, 2000).

VALLENTIN, Antonina: *Picasso.* Ed. Albin Michel (Paris, 1957).

WIDMAIER, Olivier: *Picasso, portraits de famille* (Paris, 2003).

ARTICLES AND OTHER PUBLICATIONS

ALAMEDA, Sol: *La generosidad de los herederos.* EPS, País semanal, núm. 1412 (Madrid, 19 octubre 2003).

ALCAIDE, Soledad: *Picasso inédito.* El País (Madrid, 9 mayo 2004).

ANDREU, Pierre: *Destinée de Max Jacob.* La Nation Française. Núm. 342. (Paris, 25 Avril 1962).

BATET, Estel: *Palau Fabre amplia la Fundació amb Picasso.* Avui (Barcelona, 26-XI-2003).

BEJARANO, José: *Picasso vuelve a casa.* La Vanguardia (Barcelona, 26 octubre 2003).

CABALLERO, Óscar: *La Pinacothèque de Paris abre con 80 Picassos de la esposa del pintor.* La Vanguardia (Barceloa, 6 novembre 2003).

— *El Museo Picasso de Paris reúne al pintor con Ingres, su inspirador.* La Vanguardia (Barcelona, 26 marzo 2004).

CASTELLAR-GASSOL, J.: *Art català al món.* Projecció exterior. Generalitat de Catalunya (Barcelona, abril 2003).

— *El revival de Santiago Rusiñol.* Notícies de la Generalitat de Catalunya, núm.134 (Barcelona, novembre 1997).

— *Hospital español del arte*. Selecciones del Reader's Digest (Madrid, abril 1971).

— *50 años de Modernismo*. Indice (Madrid, 1967).

COIGNARD, Jacqueline: *Picasso, vos papiers!*. Libération (Paris, 16 avril 2004).

COWLING, Elizabeth: *Not quite Madame Picasso*. Times Literary Supplement (London, November 2, 2001).

FABIANI, Martin: *Ambroise Vollard, bon génie des génies inconnus*. Sélection du Reader's Digest. (Paris, Janvier 1969).

FERMINGIER, André: *Pablo Picasso. 1881-1973*. Encyclopaedia Universalis. Corpus 18 (Paris, 1970).

FERNÁNDEZ-SANTOS, Elsa: *En defensa de Picasso*. El Pais (Madrid, 11 febrero 2004).

FERRÀS BOIX, Joaquim: *Visita a Picasso*. Centre Picasso d'Hort i Centre d'Estudis de la Terra Alta (Horta de Sant Joan, 1995).

FOIX, Josep Vicenç: *Aspectes del feixisme: l'expressió d'una voluntat nacional*. La Publicitat (Barcelona, 2 juliol 1924).

FRISACH, Montse: *Picasso, l'avi terriblement meravellós*. Avui (Barcelona, 11 febrer 2004).

GASTON MEMBRADO, Elias: *Picasso torna a Horta*. Centre Picasso d'Horta (Horta de Sant Joan, 1995).

JIMÉNEZ-BLANCO, Maria D.: *Picasso transforma Malaga*. Culturas. La Vanguardia, Barcelona (26-XI-2003).

JOLY, Pierre: *De Renoir à Picasso*. La Nouvelle critique. Núm.57 (Paris, Juillet-Août, 1954).

JUNYER VIDAL, Carlos: *Picasso y su obra*. El Liberal (Madrid, 24 marzo 1904).

LORD, James: *Stalin's painter*. The Times Literary Supplement (London, March 30, 2001).

MANGAN, Sherry: *L'Affaire Picasso*. Time Magazine (New York, 30 October 1944).

Martínez, Ignacio: *Malaga recupera todos los estilos de Picasso*. El País (Madrid, 28 octubre 2003).

Martínez de Pisón, Javier: *El arte norteamericano está infectado. Entrevista con Robert Hughes*. El País (Madrid, 11 febrero 1995).

Masoliver Martínez, Juan Ramón: *Possibilitats i hipocresia del surrealisme d'Espanya*. Butlletí de l'Agrupament Escolar de l'Acadèmia i Laboratori de Ciències Mèdiques de Catalunya. Núm. 7-9 (Barcelona, juliol-setembre 1930).

McCully, Marilyn: *Picasso*. The New Encyclopaedia Britannica. Macropaedia. 15th Edition (Chicago, USA, 1993).

Morice, Charles: *Exposition*. Mercure de France (Paris, décembre 1902).

Navarro, Justo: *Malaga en 1881*. EPS, País semanal, núm. 1412 (Madrid, 19 octubre 2003).

Palau i Fabre, Josep: *Picasso i Horta*. Centre Picasso d'Horta i Centre d'Estudis de la Terra Alta. (Horta de Sant Joan, 1995).

Pozzi, Sandro: «*Muchacho con pipa», de Picasso, el cuadro más caro de la historia*. El País (Madrid, 6 mayo 2004).

Richardson, John: *Picasso's Apocaliptic Whorehouse*. The New York Review of Books. Vol. 34. Num. 7 (New York, April 233, 1987).

Robinson, Andy: *Un Picasso de récord*. La Vanguardia (Barcelona, 4 May 2004).

Ródenas de Moia, Domingo: *Los vasos comunicantes de la radicalidad de la vanguardia y el fascismo*. Quaderns de Vallençana. Núm.1. (Montcada i Reixac, juny 2003).

Ruiz, V. J., and Fornós, T.: *Terra Alta*. Departament de Comerç, Consum i Turisme. Generalitat de Catalunya (Barcelona, 1988).

S.S.(sense signatura): *Picasso, sospechoso en Paris*. Historia y
vida, núm. 424 (Barcelona, 2003).

TALITZKY, Boris: *Jeuneusse de Picasso*. Les Lettres Françaises.
Núm. 521 (Paris, 17 juin 1954).

UTRILLO, Miquel («Pinzell»): *Dibuixos d'en Picasso*. Pèl i Ploma (Barcelona, juny 1901).

* * *

PARIS par arrondissements. Cartes Taride (Paris, 1954).
Encyclopaedia Universalis (Paris).
The New Encyclopaedia Britannica (Chicago, 1993).
Gran Enciclopèdia Catalana (Barcelona, 1969-1993).
Diccionari de tècniques pictòriques. De Jordi Gumí i Ramon
Lluís Monllaó. Ed. 62 (Barcelona, 1988).

MUSEUMS AND CENTRES
WITH WORKS BY PICASSO

FRANCE
  Musée Picasso, PARIS
  Musée Picasso, ANTIBES
  Musée National Picasso, VALLAURIS
  Museu d'Art Modern, CERET
  Musée National d'Art Moderne, Centre G. Pompidou, PARIS

CATALUNYA
  Museu Picasso, BARCELONA
  Centre Picasso, HORTA DE SANT JOAN
  Museu del Cau Ferrat, SITGES
  Museu de Montserrat, Abadia, MONTSERRAT

SPAIN
  Museo Picasso, MALAGA
  Casón del Buen Retiro, Prado, MADRID
  Museo Nacional Centro de Arte Reina Sofía, MADRID

USA

MOMA (Museum of Modern Art), NEW YORK
Solomon R. Guggenheim Museum, NEW YORK
Metropolitan Museum of Art, NEW YORK
Cleveland Museum of Art, CLEVELAND
Art Institute, CHICAGO
National Gallery of Art, WASHINGTON, D.C.
Albright-Knox Art Gallery, BUFFALO
Philadelphia Museum of Art, PHILADELPHIA
Daley Center Plaza. CHICAGO

CANADA

Art Gallery of Ontario, ONTARIO

GERMANY

Staatsgalerie, STUTTGART
Ludwig Museum, KÖLN
Kuntssammlung Nordrhein-Westfalen, DÜSSELDORF
Städelsches Kunstinstitut, FRANKFURT

SWITZERLAND

Kuntsmuseum, BASEL
Am Rhyn-Haus, LUZERN
Kunstmuseum, BERN

RUSSIA
Hermitage, SANT PETERSBURG
Puxkin Museum, MOSCOW

SERBIA
Museu Nacional, BELGRAD

Theczch Republi
Narodni Galerie, PRAGA

Great Britain
Tate Gallery, LONDON

Sweden
Moderna Museet, STOCKHOLM
Göteborgs Kuntsmuseum, GÖTEBORG

Brazil
Museu de Arte, SÄO PAULO
Museu de Arte Moderna, RIO DE JANEIRO

The Museum Picasso of Barcelona

The Museu Picasso de Barcelona, which holds the majority of the artist's early works —more than 3,600— is considered the most important and complete of its genre in the world. It was also the first museum in the world to open with the artist's name. The works held are mostly oil paintings and coloured pictures in diverse media but also include prints and ceramics.

Founded in 1963, the museum presently occupies an exceptional space in the medieval Montcada Street, in the gothic quarter of the Catalan capital, a space made up of six houses of ancient origin, although they have been restored and to some extent remodelled throughout time. The Palau Aguilar —also called the Palau Caldes— dates from the 12th and 13th centuries. The Palau Finestres dates from the 13th century. The Palau del Baró de Castellet, and the Palau Meca date from the 14th and 15th centuries. The Casa Mauri, which formed part of the Palau Meca, dates from the 18th century. As a whole these buildings form a harmonic architectural whole which merits a visit in its own right. In fact, in recent years it has been one of the most important centres of world tourism.

THE MUSEUM PICASSO OF MÁLAGA

The Museo Picasso Málaga exhibits a collection of 155 works by Pablo Picasso, which were donated and lent by Christine and Bernard Ruiz-Picasso, the artist's daughter-in-law and grandson respectively.

This donation and the initiatives taken by the regional government of Andalusia made possible the creation of the Museum, located in the old heart of the city, in the Palacio de Buenavista, a venerable building of the first half of the sixteenth century. This historical building and other aspects adjacent to the new constructions integrate a whole of more than 8,000 square metres.

Málaga is one of the oldest cities in Occident and it is not surprising that its subsoil is extremely rich in archaeological sites. Underneath the Palace, the remains of Phoenician dwellings and walls of the seventh and sixth centuries BC can be visited.

The Museo Picasso Málaga is, therefore, a double attraction for tourists or visitors.

J. Castellar-Gassol is a member of the AELC (Association of writers in the Catalan language), a branch of the EWC (European Writers Congress). He lives and works in Barcelona. He has published, among others, biographies of Gaudí, Jacint Verdaguer and Dalí.

OTHER SUCCESSFUL BOOKS
BY JOAN CASTELLAR-GASSOL

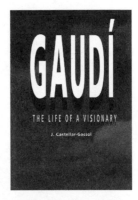